JESUS THE
SON OF GOD

JESUS THE SON OF GOD

A Christological Title Often Overlooked,
Sometimes Misunderstood,
and Currently Disputed

D. A. Carson

CROSSWAY

WHEATON, ILLINOIS

Trade paperback ISBN: 978-1-4335-3796-7
PDF ISBN: 978-1-4335-3797-4
Mobipocket ISBN: 978-1-4335-3798-1
ePub ISBN: 978-1-4335-3799-8

Library of Congress Cataloging-in-Publication Data

Carson, D. A.
   Jesus the Son of God : a christological title often
      overlooked, sometimes misunderstood, and currently
      disputed / D.A. Carson.
      p. cm.
   Includes bibliographical references and indexes.
   ISBN 978-1-4335-3796-7
   1. Jesus Christ—Divinity. 2. Son of God. I. Title.
BT216.3.C37   2012
232'.8—dc23   2012021031

Crossway is a publishing ministry of Good News Publishers.

VP		21	20	19	18	17	16	15	14	13	12
15	14	13	12	11	10	9	8	7	6	5	4	3	2	1

"No christological designation is as essential as 'Son of God'; none is more important. This study makes that impressively clear by sound and careful exegesis and theological reflection in the face of misunderstandings and disputes, past and current. Once again, D. A. Carson serves the church well."

> **Richard B. Gaffin Jr.**, Professor of Biblical and Systematic Theology, Emeritus, Westminster Theological Seminary

"I know what it is to reject Jesus as the 'Son of God.' As a former Muslim, nothing baffled and, quite frankly, angered me more than hearing Christians call Jesus 'the Son of God.' I thought such persons were blasphemers worthy of condemnation. But now, nothing gives me more joy than to know that Jesus is indeed the Son of God and that the title 'Son of God' carries far more truth and wonder than I could have imagined. So I welcome this volume from D. A. Carson with all the enthusiasm and joy of one who once denied the truth that Jesus is the Son of God. With his customarily clear, warm, careful, and balanced manner, Carson gives us a fresh exploration of a precious truth that so many Christians take for granted and so many Muslims misunderstand. If you want to know Jesus and the Bible better, this surely is one aid that will not disappoint."

> **Thabiti Anyabwile**, Senior Pastor, First Baptist Church of Grand Cayman; author, *What Is a Healthy Church Member?*

"What does it mean for us to confess that Jesus is the Son of God? D. A. Carson tackles this question in *Jesus the Son of God*. In this little book he lays a firm foundation to help the church understand 'Son of God' with reference to Jesus. After considering uses of 'Son of God' in Scripture, both in general and when applied to Jesus, Carson models the way systematic theology should be based on solid biblical exegesis. Carson is especially concerned to bring his study to bear on the controverted issue in missiological circles concerning how to present Jesus as Son of God in Christian and Muslim contexts. Here he critically, but kindly, calls for rethinking new translations that have replaced references to God the Father and Jesus as his Son to make them more acceptable to Muslims."

> **Robert A. Peterson**, Professor of Systematic Theology, Covenant Seminary

This book is gratefully dedicated to
John Piper
who keeps reminding us by his own practice
to pay attention to the text.

CONTENTS

PREFACE

This little book originated in three lectures delivered at Reformed Theological Seminary in Jackson, Mississippi, on March 5–6, 2012. In shortened form it became the Gaffin Lecture on Theology, Culture, and Mission at Westminster Theological Seminary on March 14, 2012, and then, slightly modified, became the substance of three lectures in French at the Colloque Réformée held in Lyon, France, in April of the same year. I am enormously indebted to Michel Lemaire and Jacob Mathieu for their very careful work of translation. It is a pleasure rather than a mere obligation to express my hearty gratitude to those who organized these lectures and invited me to participate. I am hugely indebted to them for their hospitality and kindness.

I chose the topic about three years ago. Some work I had done while teaching the epistle to the Hebrews, especially Hebrews 1 where Jesus is said to be superior to angels because he is the Son, prompted me to think about the topic more globally. Moreover, for some time I have been thinking through the hiatus between careful exegesis and doctrinal formulations. We need both, of course, but unless the latter are finally controlled by the former, and *seen* to be controlled by the former, both are weakened. The "Son of God" theme has become one of several test cases in my own mind. Since choosing the topic, however, the debates concerning what a faithful translation of "Son of God" might be, especially in contexts where one's envisioned readers are Muslims, have boiled out of the journals read by Bible translators and into the open. Entire denominations have gotten caught up in the controversy, which shows no sign of abating. The last of these three chapters is devoted to addressing both of these points—how, in a Christian context, exegesis rightly leads to Christian confessionalism, and how, in a cross-cultural context concerned with preparing Bible translations for Muslim readers, one may wisely negotiate the current debate. But I beg you to read the first two chapters first. They provide the necessary textual detail on which discussion of the controversies must be based.

This book is not meant to be primarily a contribution to the current disputes, as important as those debates may be. It is meant to foster clear thinking among Christians who want to know what we mean when we join believers across the centuries in confessing, "I believe in God the Father Almighty, Maker of heaven and earth, and in his only Son Jesus, our Lord."

Once again it is a pleasure to record my indebtedness to Andy Naselli for his invaluable suggestions.

Soli Deo gloria.

CHAPTER ONE

"SON OF GOD" AS A CHRISTOLOGICAL TITLE

"I believe in God the Father Almighty, Maker of heaven and earth, and in his only Son Jesus, our Lord." Millions of Christians recite these words from the Apostles' Creed week by week. But what does it mean to confess Jesus as God's only Son? What does it mean to say that the God of the Bible has a Son? It cannot possibly mean exactly the same thing that I mean when I tell people, "Yes, I have a son." Moreover, here and there in Scripture we learn (as we shall see) that Adam is God's son, Israel is God's son, King Solomon is God's son, the Israelites are sons of God, the peacemakers shall be called sons of God, and angels can be referred to as God's sons. So in what way is Jesus's sonship like, or unlike, any of these? Why should we think of him as God's *only* Son?

PRELIMINARY REFLECTIONS

For at least a century, Christian preaching and writing have focused much more attention on Jesus's deity and Jesus's lordship than on Jesus's sonship. In recent times, when Christians have written and spoken about Jesus as the Son of God, they have tended to focus on one of three topics.

First, many works forged within the discipline of systematic theology discuss the sonship of Jesus, and especially the title "Son of God," within their broader treatment of Trinitarian theology. The volume by Alister McGrath offers no "Son of God" entry in its index.[1] When Professor McGrath treats "the biblical foundations of the Trinity," he mentions three "personifications" of God within the Bible (though he prefers the term "hypostatizations"), namely, wisdom, the Word of God, and the Spirit of God.[2] "Son" is not mentioned. But McGrath nicely treats the "Son" in the ensuing pages that work through the historical development of the doctrine of the Trinity during the patristic period. Here readers learn the Eastern approach to the Trinity (the Father begets the Son and breathes or "spirates" the Holy Spirit) and the Western approach to the Trinity (the Father begets the Son, and Father and Son breathe the Holy Spirit).[3] McGrath devotes almost no effort to tying these discussions down to what the *biblical* texts actually say: this part of his treatment is caught up in patristic controversies. The recent and fine work of systematic theology by Michael Horton, in keeping with its greater length, devotes much more space to the Trinity, including more effort to tie his theological conclusions to Scripture.[4] Yet neither McGrath nor Horton works through the different ways in which the title "Son of God" applies to Jesus. They focus almost exclusively on passages in which "Son of

---

[1] Alister McGrath, *Christian Theology: An Introduction* (Oxford, UK: Blackwell, 1994).
[2] Ibid., 248–49.
[3] Here, of course, McGrath includes a brief treatment of the *filioque* controversy: does the Holy Spirit proceed "from the Father" only (the agreed terminology of the Nicene Creed) or "from the Father *and the Son*" (captured in Latin by the *filioque*)? The Western church insisted on the latter addition.
[4] Michael Horton, *The Christian Faith: A Systematic Theology for Pilgrims on the Way* (Grand Rapids, MI: Zondervan, 2011).

God" applies to Jesus *and appears to have some bearing on our understanding of the Trinity.* That is understandable, even commendable, granted their projects. Nevertheless, it leaves readers in the dark about the diversity of ways in which "Son of God" is used to refer to Jesus, and about the ways in which the same "son" language can be applied to Adam, Israelites, Solomon, peacemakers, and angels.[5] And this list is not exhaustive!

Second, a handful of works are specialist volumes focusing not on the categories of systematic theology but on slightly different lines. Sam Janse traces the reception history of Psalm 2, especially the "You are My Son" formula in early Judaism and in the New Testament.[6] The history Janse reconstructs is minimalist; certainly he draws no lines toward Trinitarianism. Following a rather different procedure, Michael Peppard analyzes the adoptive procedures in the social and political contexts of the Roman world and reads the New Testament and developing patristic evidence against that background.[7] Readers will not be entirely mistaken if they conclude that his thesis is a new reductionism, one more example of exegesis by appeals to ostensible parallels (in this case, Graeco-Roman parallels)—of "parallelomania," to use the lovely term coined by Samuel Sandmel.[8]

Third, in the last few years two spirited controversies

---

[5] One might usefully add here the few pages devoted to "Son of God" in the finely reasoned book by K. Scott Oliphint, *God with Us: Divine Condescension and the Attributes of God* (Wheaton, IL: Crossway, 2012).

[6] Sam Janse, *"You Are My Son": The Reception History of Psalm 2 in Early Judaism and the Early Church,* Contributions to Biblical Exegesis and Theology (Leuven, BE: Peeters, 2009).

[7] Michael Peppard, *The Son of God in the Roman World: Divine Sonship in Its Social and Political Context* (Oxford, UK: Oxford University Press, 2011).

[8] Samuel Sandmel, "Parallelomania," *Journal of Biblical Literature* 81 (1962): 2–13.

have erupted and garnered their share of publications regarding "Son" or "Son of God" terminology applied to Jesus. The first of these clashes concerns the extent to which the Son is or is not subordinate to the Father, with a correlative bearing on debates over egalitarianism and complementarianism. I shall not devote much time to that debate in these chapters, but merely offer a handful of observations along the way. The second clash debates how the expression "Son of God" should be translated, especially in Bible translations designed for the Muslim world. I shall devote part of the third chapter to that subject—but I shall be prepared to do so only after laying the groundwork in the first two chapters.

These, then, have been the three major foci of interest when "Son of God" has been probed in recent years. Interesting exceptions occasionally surface. For example, one thinks of the recent excellent volume by Robert A. Peterson, *Salvation Accomplished by the Son: The Work of Christ*.[9] Despite its many strengths, however, it says relatively little about how the Son-language *works* as applied to Jesus— that is, what it actually *means*. One may charitably suppose that this is primarily because Peterson's focus is on the *work* of Christ rather than on the *person* of Christ. Again, the uniquely arranged and massive biblical theology of Greg Beale devotes many pages to Jesus's sonship.[10] Precisely because he is interested in tracing out developing trajectories through the Bible, Beale's treatment is often much more tightly bound to specific biblical texts and less interested in

---

[9] Robert A. Peterson, *Salvation Accomplished by the Son: The Work of Christ* (Wheaton, IL: Crossway, 2012).
[10] G. K. Beale, *A New Testament Biblical Theology: The Unfolding of the Old Testament in the New* (Grand Rapids, MI: Baker, 2011), esp. 316–19, 400–429, 441–43, 670–72, 704–8, 761, 913–15.

later theological controversies that developed their own specialist terminology.

In the rest of this chapter, I focus first on sons and sonship, then on son or sons of God where there is no undisputed link with Jesus as the unique Son, and finally on Jesus the Son of God. I shall not restrict the discussion to passages where "son" or "sons" occur: after all, if God is portrayed as the Father, then in some sense those who are in relationship with him are being thought of as his sons or his children.

SONS AND SONSHIP

A large majority of the occurrences of "son" in the Bible, whether singular or plural but without the modifier "of God," refer to a biological son. Sometimes the son is named: "When [Boaz] made love to [Ruth], the LORD enabled her to conceive, and she gave birth to a son. . . . And they named him Obed" (Ruth 4:13, 17); "Then God said, 'Take your son, your only son, whom you love—Isaac—and go to the region of Moriah. Sacrifice him there as a burnt offering on a mountain I will show you'" (Gen. 22:2). Sometimes the son, unnamed in the immediate context, is identified with a patronymic: "I have seen a son of Jesse of Bethlehem who knows how to play the lyre" (1 Sam. 16:18); or frequent references in the New Testament to the sons of Zebedee. If not the patronymic, there may be some other identifier, for example, "the son of Pharaoh's daughter" (Heb. 11:24) or "the carpenter's son" (Matt. 13:55).[11] At other times the son is not named, but the context shows the relationship envis-

---

[11] Of course, in this instance Jesus is not biologically the son of a carpenter, but in the mind of the speakers he is. At this juncture I am interested only in language usage.

aged is entirely natural, as when the Shunammite woman berates Elisha, "Did I ask you for a son, my lord?" (2 Kings 4:28). This usage is very common: for example, "[Ahaz] followed the ways of the kings of Israel and even sacrificed his son in the fire" (2 Kings 16:3); "When it was time for Elizabeth to have her baby, she gave birth to a son" (Luke 1:57)—and of course the context soon discloses the son's name, John (1:63). Under this usage are the occasions when a parent addresses a child, whose name is known, with the word "son," as when Mary says to Jesus, "Son, why have you treated us like this? Your father and I have been anxiously searching for you" (Luke 2:48).

Sometimes the context shows that the word "son" is not referring to an individual, named or otherwise, but to a class, a typical son, as it were: "Know then in your heart that as a man disciplines his son, so the LORD your God disciplines you" (Deut. 8:5); "But suppose this son has a son who sees all the sins his father commits, and though he sees them, he does not do such things" (Ezek. 18:14). This kind of usage is scarcely less frequent in the New Testament: "Anyone who loves their son or daughter more than me is not worthy of me" (Matt. 10:37); "There was a man who had two sons" (Luke 15:11). Perhaps this is also the place to mention passages where "son" is used, not to address an immediately male biological descendant, but a more distant relative, a member of the larger clan or tribe who is considerably younger—almost an avuncular usage, as when, in the story of the rich man and Lazarus, Abraham addresses the rich man as he suffers torments in Hades, "Son, remember . . ." (Luke 16:25).

All the examples mentioned so far presuppose natural sonship, biological sonship, as opposed to metaphorical usage. Before turning to the extensive metaphorical use of "son" and related terms in the Bible, it will prove helpful to reflect on what many of the expressions I am about to list have in common. In contemporary Western culture, sonship is established irrefutably by DNA: the biological connection can be established scientifically within a minuscule margin of error. By extension we also speak of adopted sons: the biological link disappears from view, but the legal and familial ties are very strong. What we are *not* used to are expressions like "sons of affliction," "son of the morning," "son of a bow," and a host of others I shall list—all of them found in Scripture, though mostly unpreserved in contemporary translations. What do they have in common?

Vocationally speaking, in our culture relatively few sons end up doing what their fathers did; relatively few daughters end up doing what their mothers did. In many contexts I have asked this question: "How many of you men are now doing, vocationally, what your fathers did at the same age? How many of you women are now doing, vocationally, what your mothers did at the same age?" The percentage is rarely as much as 5 percent. In the ancient world, however, the percentage would have been much higher, frequently well over 90 percent. If your father was a farmer, you became a farmer; if your father was a baker, you became a baker; if your father was a carpenter, you became a carpenter—which of course is why Jesus could be known both as the carpenter's son (Matt. 13:55), and, in one remarkable passage, as the carpenter (Mark 6:3—presumably after Joseph had died). If your family name was Stradivarius, you became a violin maker. You learned your trade, your vocation, even your identity, *from your father*. If you were a farmer, you learned *from your father* when and how to plant, when and how to irrigate, when and how to harvest—not from a nearby agricultural college. If you made violins, you learned *from your father* what woods to choose, what sizes and ratios each piece had to maintain, what glues to use, and how to make and apply the finish. To put the matter differently, your father determined your identity, your training, your vocation. He generated you not only biologically, but, shall we say, functionally. You were derived from him, not only biologically, but functionally. Transparently, this father-son relationship works only one way: the son does not generate the father, biologically or functionally, nor does the son give his identity to the father.

In other words, your paternity was responsible for much more than your genes; your father provided much more than school fees. He established your vocation, your place in the culture, your identity, your place in the family. This is the dynamic of a culture that is preindustrial and fundamentally characterized by agriculture, handcrafts, and small-time trade.

This social dynamic does not necessarily shape the linguistic structures of all cultures characterized by it, but it certainly does the Hebrew culture. As a result there are many "son of X" idioms in the Bible, where the identity of "X" is highly diverse and the relationship between the son and X is certainly not biological.

Consider, for example, the expression "son(s) of Belial," or "men [or occasionally 'daughter'] of Belial," where "Belial" is usually masked by contemporary translations:

Chart 1

Text	KJV	NIV	ESV
Deut. 13:13	the children of Belial	troublemakers	worthless fellows
Judg. 19:22	certain sons of Belial	some of the wicked men	worthless fellows
Judg. 20:13	the children of Belial	those wicked men	the worthless fellows
1 Sam. 1:16	a daughter of Belial	a wicked woman	a worthless woman
1 Sam. 2:12	sons of Belial	scoundrels	worthless men
1 Sam. 10:27	the children of Belial	some scoundrels	some worthless fellows
1 Sam. 25:17	a son of Belial	such a wicked man	such a worthless man
1 Sam. 25:25	this man of Belial	that wicked man	this worthless fellow
1 Sam. 30:22	the wicked men and men of Belial	the evil men and troublemakers	the wicked and worthless fellows
2 Sam. 16:7	thou man of Belial	you scoundrel	you worthless man
2 Sam. 20:1	a man of Belial	a troublemaker	a worthless man
2 Sam. 23:6	the sons of Belial	evil men	worthless men
1 Kings 21:10	sons of Belial	scoundrels	worthless men
1 Kings 21:13	children of Belial	scoundrels	worthless men
2 Chron. 13:7	vain men, the children of Belial	worthless scoundrels	worthless scoundrels
2 Cor. 6:15	And what concord hath Christ with Belial?	What harmony is there between Christ and Belial?	What accord has Christ with Belial?

A few observations will draw attention to salient points. (1) The word "Belial" is preserved as a transliteration from the Hebrew, and in the last instance, from the

Greek,[12] in every occurrence in the KJV. It is preserved by both the NIV and the ESV in only one passage, namely, the last—that is, in the one passage where there is no "son of" or "man of" locution to introduce it, where "Christ" is set over against "Belial." (2) Apart from this last instance, the ESV consistently understands the "of Belial" component to mean "worthless." That may be right, but it is not certainly so; it is in line with one of four or five commonly suggested derivations of the word "Belial." In the last instance, Paul uses "Belial" as a synonym for Satan. (3) Calling someone "a son of Belial" is not necessarily suggesting that the *biological* father of the son is Belial/worthless/wicked/a scoundrel/Satan. Rather, it is a dramatic way of saying that the conduct of the son is so worthless/wicked that he is identified with the worthless/wicked family. That is his identity. (4) There is probably little difference between "son of Belial" and "man of Belial." In both cases "Belial" identifies the son's or the man's character and conduct. If there is a difference between the two expressions, "son of Belial" calls up a mental image of "Belial" *generating* the son, while "man of Belial," though it identifies the man with Belial, conjures up no image of Belial generating the man. (5) Neither the NIV nor the ESV attempts to preserve the "son of" or "daughter of" component of the expression.

There is a substantial number of other "son(s) of X" expressions in the Bible that only rarely get translated in such a way as to preserve the "son(s) of" component. The following list is not exhaustive but is broadly comprehensive:

---

[12] There is, of course, a well-known textual variant here, "Beliar."

Chart 2

Text	Literal Rendering	KJV	NIV	ESV
Ex. 12:5	son of one year	a male of the first year	year-old males	a male a year old
Deut. 25:2	sons of the beating	worthy to be beaten	deserves to be beaten	deserves to be beaten
2 Sam. 17:10	sons of might	a mighty man	a fighter	a mighty man
2 Kings 6:32	son of a murder	son of a murder	murderer	murderer
2 Kings 16:7	your son [i.e., a king subordinate to another king]	your son	your vassal	your son
Neh. 12:28	sons of the singers	sons of the singers	musicians	sons of the singers
Job 5:7	sons of a flame	sparks	sparks	sparks
Job 41:28	son of a bow	arrow	arrows	arrow
Ps. 89:22	son of malice	the son of wickedness	the wicked	the wicked
Ps. 149:2	sons of Zion	the children of Zion	the people of Zion	the children of Zion
Prov. 31:5	sons of affliction	the afflicted	the oppressed	the afflicted
Isa. 14:12	son of the morning	son of the morning	son of the dawn	son of Dawn
Isa. 19:11	son of wise men	son of the wise	wise counselors	son of the wise
Isa. 21:10	sons of the threshing floor [i.e., threshed corn]	O my threshing and the corn of my floor	My people who are crushed on the threshing floor	O my threshed and winnowed one
Isa. 57:3	sons of a fortune-teller	ye sons of the sorceress	you children of a sorceress	sons of the sorceress
Lam. 3:13	sons of the quiver	arrows of his quiver	arrows from his quiver	arrows of his quiver

Zech. 4:14	sons of oil	anointed ones	who are anointed	anointed ones
Matt. 13:38	sons of the kingdom	children of the kingdom	people of the kingdom	sons of the kingdom
Matt. 13:38	sons of the evil one	children of the wicked one	people of the evil one	sons of the evil one
Matt. 17:25	sons [of kings]	their own [kings'] children	their own [kings'] children	their [kings'] sons
Mark 2:19	sons of the bridechamber	children of the bridechamber	guests of the bridegroom	the wedding guests

Once again a few observations will clarify the significance of the chart.

(1) In the expression "son(s) of X," the "X" is often abstract, or at least nonpersonal, nonhuman (e.g., son of one year, sons of affliction, son of morning, sons of oil, sons of the quiver). In all such cases, the relationship between the "son" and "X" cannot, of course, be biological. Even where "X" is a person, the relationship is not, in these examples, biological. The "son of wise men" does not refer to the literal progeny of wise men; it refers, rather, to those whose conduct and counsel are so wise that they are identified, as it were, with the company of the wise, with the wise family: that is their family, their identity. The sons of a fortune-teller are not her literal children; they are, rather, those who go to fortune-tellers for guidance, and thus show themselves to belong to those who cherish fortune-telling.

(2) The exact nuance of the relationship between the "son" and the "X" is highly variable. The "sons of the beating" (Deut. 25:2) refers to those who *deserve* to be beaten, that is, they deserve to be punished; they belong to that class.

By contrast, the "sons of a flame" do not *deserve* a flame; rather, the entire expression metaphorically conjures up sparks. Ordinarily the exact nuance is easily discernible from the context. Sometimes there is a sense of the "X" generating the "son": for example, the flame generates the spark.

(3) In some instances, to preserve a more direct rendering in English is distinctly misleading. The ESV preserves "sons of the singers" in Nehemiah 12:28, and an untutored English reader might well take this to refer to the biological progeny of singers. In fact, the reference is to singers, musicians—not their progeny.

(4) "Sons of the bridechamber" (Mark 2:19) is particularly interesting. Both the NIV and the ESV recognize that the expression refers to guests at a wedding, but each handles the "X" component of the expression, the bridechamber, in a different way. Recognizing who issued the invitations in a first-century Jewish wedding in Palestine, NIV renders the expressions "guests of the bridegroom." The ESV in this instance adopts the more contemporary and colloquial expression, "wedding guests." Both, of course, have lost any hint of a literal bridechamber. The bridechamber does not in any sense, metaphorical or otherwise, *generate* the "sons," but it does establish the identity of these "sons."

(5) In any case, all three translations recognize that at least some of the time the most direct rendering is inappropriate. A reader can on occasion discern that the translators recognize they are dealing with a slightly alien idiom: their interpretive wrestlings may issue in an orthographic convention not available in the original language (hence the ESV's

"son of Dawn" [Isa. 14:12], with a capital letter, instead of the more prosaic "son of the morning").

This sort of background is what makes a number of other expressions in the Bible more readily comprehensible. Who are the sons of Abraham? The true sons of Abraham, Paul insists, are not those who carry Abraham's genes, but those who act like him, who imitate the faith of Abraham (Gal. 3:7; cf. John 8:33, 39–40), the "man of faith" (Gal. 3:9). The obligation of a son to imitate his father surfaces very movingly when Paul tells his converts in Corinth, "Even if you had ten thousand guardians in Christ, you do not have many fathers, for in Christ Jesus I became your father through the gospel. Therefore I urge you to imitate me" (1 Cor. 4:15–16).

One final observation before wrapping up this section. Sometimes quite different uses of "son of X" language can be found in the same passage. For example, in 1 Samuel 20:30 we read, "Saul's anger flared up at Jonathan and he said to him, 'You son of a perverse and rebellious woman![13] Don't I know that you have sided with the son of Jesse to your own shame and to the shame of the mother who bore you?'" Here the first of the two expressions, "son of a perverse and rebellious woman," is not saying anything about Jonathan's biological

---

[13] This or something similar is how the Hebrew expression is rendered by KJV, NKJV, RSV, NRSV, NASB, ESV, HCSB, and NIV. The NET Bible has "You stupid traitor!" and appends the following note: "*Heb* 'son of a perverse woman of rebelliousness.' But such an overly literal and domesticated translation of the Hebrew expression fails to capture the force of Saul's unrestrained reaction. Saul, now incensed and enraged over Jonathan's liaison with David, is actually hurling very coarse and emotionally charged words at his son. The translation of this phrase suggested by Ludwig Koehler and Walter Baumgartner is 'bastard of a wayward woman' (*Hebrew and Aramaic Lexicon of the Old Testament,* s.v. הוע), but this is not an expression commonly used in English. A better English approximation of the sentiments expressed here by the Hebrew phrase would be 'You stupid son of a bitch!' However, sensitivity to the various public formats in which the Bible is read aloud has led to a less startling English rendering which focuses on the semantic value of Saul's utterance (i.e., the behavior of his own son Jonathan, which he viewed as both a personal and a political betrayal [= 'traitor'])." Cf. NLT: "You stupid son of a whore!"; *The Message*: "You son of a slut!"

mother. If that were so, why would King Saul imagine, in the second part of the verse, that Jonathan's actions would bring shame on her? In the second of the two expressions, "son of Jesse," the sonship is at lone level unavoidably biological, yet the searing sneer in King Saul's voice suggests he is not opting to refer to David merely by referencing his patronymic. Rather, he wants to damn not only David but Jesse's entire clan—or, better put perhaps, he holds that David is utterly contemptible *because* he springs from this contemptible clan. In other words, the distinctions in how "son of X" functions in the two occurrences of this text are subtle, but not really obscure once one pays attention to the flow of the argument and the nature of this metaphor.

THE USE OF "SON(S) OF GOD" TO REFER TO BEINGS OTHER THAN JESUS

We move now from a survey of "son(s) of X" expressions where "X" is anything but God, to "son(s) of X" expressions where X is God. I shall include some instances where, for example, God is portrayed as the Father who has sons, even though the precise expression "son(s) of God" is not used. On the other hand, I shall exclude instances where "son of God" is clearly christological,[14] reserving such passages for

---

[14] I am using "christological" in a fairly broad sense to include references to the one who comes to be named Jesus. This awkward way of putting things stems from the fact that the terminology is a bit tricky. For example, if I had said, more simply, "to include references to Jesus" instead of "to include references to the one who comes to be named Jesus," I would be excluding Old Testament references to the Coming One for no other reason than that he is not yet named Jesus. Again, "christological" is itself awkward because, at its basic level, it is simply a Greek version of the Hebrew "messianic." But as we shall see, there are numerous passages where "son of God" is tied to the promised Davidic Messiah (hence this is a messianic usage of "son of God"), and others where "son of God" is tied to a coming figure who is not in that context connected with the Davidic Messiah (hence this is a nonmessianic usage of "son of God"). Both kinds of usages we shall nevertheless label christological, provided "son of God" refers to the Coming One (however he is understood in any passage), whether before he comes as the man Jesus, or once he is here.

the next two chapters. The immediate aim is to remind our-selves that in the Bible "son(s) of God" can refer to a diverse range of beings—a fact we may overlook because "son of God" is so tightly tied, for many of us, almost exclusively to the second person of the Godhead. Technical introductions to this diversity are found in many of the better biblical and theological dictionaries.[15] Here I intend to do no more than survey the range.

Most of the entries in this section refer to human beings, but a handful of entries clearly refer to angels. "One day the angels [*Heb.*: 'the sons of God'] came to present themselves before the LORD, and Satan also came with them" (Job 1:6; see also 2:1; 38:7). "Sons of God" is found in the original of Psalms 29:1 and 89:6; both NIV and ESV render the Hebrew "heavenly beings" rather than "sons of God." Unfallen angels, one supposes, reflect God's character in many ways. In vari-ous passages they take on revelatory roles and carry out God's purposes. The carefully worded comment—that Satan also came with them—suggests both proximity and distance: it is not too much to infer that he should have been one with them, but at this juncture must be mentioned separately, for his purposes are malign. But for the time being we shall set to one side further mention of angels.

What, then, are the ways in which "son(s) of God" refers to human beings other than Jesus?

---

[15] See, among others, Jarl Fossum, "Son of God," in *The Anchor Bible Dictionary*, ed. David Freedman, vol. 6 (New York: Doubleday, 1992), 128–37; J. W. Drane, "Son of God," in *Dictionary of the New Testament and Its Developments*, eds. Ralph P. Martin and Peter H. Davids (Downers Grove, IL: IVP, 1997), 1111–15; D. R. Bauer, "Son of God," in *Dictionary of Jesus and the Gospels,* eds. Joel Green and Scot McKnight (Downers Grove, IL: IVP, 1992), 769–75; L. W. Hurtado, "Son of God," in *Dictionary of Paul and His Letters*, eds. Gerald F. Hawthorne, Ralph P. Martin, and Daniel G. Reid (Downers Grove, IL: IVP, 1993), 900–906.

(1) In Luke 3, the genealogy of Jesus is traced all the way back to "Adam, the son of God" (3:38). Transparently he is not the son of God in exactly the same sense that every other person in the genealogy is said to be the son of another human being. Certainly Adam is the son of God in the sense that God generated him, making him in the image and likeness of God, created to reflect God's glory—indeed, to be like him in all ways that are appropriate for human beings, male and female, to imitate God.[16] Indeed, this combined sense of derivation from God and obligation to God is applicable to all of Adam's progeny, even though God's creation of Adam is unique. After all, God made Adam directly, with no human mediation, unlike the way all later human beings come into existence. Adam's role is in several senses unique. That is why the apostle Paul, addressing the Athenian philosophers, is prepared to use the words of Aratus to make the point: We human beings are *God's offspring* (Acts 17:28)—a take on origins that the Athenians, who thought they had superior roots to all other tribes, would have found insulting.

(2) As early as Exodus 4:22–23, the singular expression "son of God" can refer to Israel collectively: Moses tells Pharaoh, "This is what the LORD says: Israel is my firstborn son, and I told you, 'Let my son go, so he may worship me.' But you refused to let him go; so I will kill your firstborn son." One might well ponder the analogical relationship between God's firstborn son and Pharaoh's firstborn son in this passage, but for the moment we press on with our survey. The same collective understanding of Israel as God's son is found

---

[16] For an excellent if brief treatment of the significance of being made "in the image of God," see C. John Collins, *Did Adam and Eve Really Exist? Why They Were and Why You Should Care* (Wheaton, IL: Crossway, 2011), 93–104.

in Psalm 80:15 ("the son you have raised up for yourself") and Hosea 11:1 ("Out of Egypt I have called my son"), even if Matthew applies this latter text to Jesus (Matt. 2:15). It lurks behind the warning Moses gives to Israel: "You forgot the God who gave you birth" (Deut. 32:18). God is quoted as saying, "I am Israel's father, and Ephraim is my firstborn son" (Jer. 31:9), thus showing that the expression "firstborn son" can be used collectively to refer to the northern tribes precisely because, however far they have fallen, they constitute part of the covenant people of God.

(3) The expression "son(s) of God" can refer to God's covenant people, individually or plurally (rather than collectively), both under the terms of the old covenant and under the terms of the new. Moses tells the Israelites, "You are the sons of the LORD your God" (Deut. 14:1, NASB and NIV; NIV has "children" instead of "sons"; see also Isa. 43:6; 45:11; 63:8; Jer. 3:19). Not dissimilarly, Paul tells the Galatian believers, "For in Christ Jesus you are all sons of God, through faith" (3:26 ESV; see also Rom. 8:14; Phil. 2:15; 1 John 3:1). Under the old covenant, God is sometimes referred to as the (heavenly) Father (e.g., Mal. 2:10); under the new covenant, believers are taught to address God as "our Father."

(4) Perhaps as a subset of this usage, or, better, a specific exemplification of it, sonship language can be applied to Christ's followers when in some way or other they are imitating God, their heavenly Father. In Matthew's version of the Beatitudes, Jesus declares, "Blessed are the peacemakers, for they will be called [lit.] the sons of God" (Matt. 5:9). These words do not tell us how to become one of Jesus's disciples. Rather, they presuppose that God is the supreme Peacemaker,

with the result that those who make peace show themselves to be, at least on that axis, members of God's peacemaking clan, as it were: they are sons of God. The thought is similar in Matthew 5:44–45, where God's propensity for showering good gifts on his enemies is held up for emulation. Another subset of believers is found in Psalm 82:6, where it appears that the leaders of Israel are designated "sons of the Most High" (though it is possible the reference is to all Israelites). Similarly, in Luke 6:35–36, Jesus says, "But love your enemies, do good to them, and lend to them without expecting to get anything back. Then your reward will be great, and you will be [lit.] sons of the Most High, because he is kind to the ungrateful and wicked. Be merciful, just as your Father is merciful." Once again it is the imitative role of sons that is assumed, along with the correlative pattern- and identity-establishing function of the father.

(5) More specifically, the Davidic king is designated the "son of God." The ultimate fount of the many passages that use "son of God" in this way is 2 Samuel 7:14. David has been expressing his desire to build a "house" for God, but God says that it will work the other way: while David wants to build a "house" (= temple) for God, God intends to build a "house" (= dynasty) for David. Transparently the argument turns in part on a pun. Nevertheless, David's son *will* build a temple (2 Sam. 7:13), and God will establish the throne of his kingdom forever. "I will be his father," God declares, "and he will be my son" (7:14a). In the context, it is not Jesus who is in view, but Solomon, for God adds, "When he does wrong, I will punish him with a rod wielded by men, with floggings inflicted by human hands" (7:14b).

Later I shall probe the connection of this passage with Jesus. For present purposes, however, it is the nature of the sonship that must be understood. God is the supreme King. When a Davidide assumes the throne, he does so under God's kingship. The reign of the Davidic king is meant to reflect God's reign, including his passion for justice, his commitment to the covenant, his hatred of idolatry, and his concern for the oppressed. As we have seen, the peacemaker may be called the son of God because he enters into the identity of the supreme Peacemaker, God himself. Similarly, the Davidic monarch is called the son of God because he enters into the identity of the supreme Monarch, God himself. Similar terminology is found in Psalm 2. God declares, "I have installed my king on Zion, my holy mountain" (2:6)—and when the Davidic king looks at this, his own installation, he proclaims the Lord's decree by proclaiming, "He said to me, 'You are my son; today I have become your father'" (2:7). This is when God "begets" him; it is at this point that the Davidide becomes God's son in this monarchical sense. Ethan the Ezrahite's vision of the appointment of David as king is similarly couched in language that makes God out to be his Father (Ps. 89:19–29). Of course, just as Satan could be included among the "sons of God" who are angels, even though he was not living up to his calling, so "son" language can be applied to wicked Davidic monarchs. In Ezekiel 21:10, for instance, God refers to the corrupt and soon-to-be-destroyed Davidic king as his "royal son."

(6) As a kind of extension of the fourth option, sonship language can be applied to believers eschatologically—that is, depicting how in the consummation the sons of God imitate their heavenly Father as perfectly as finite beings can ever imi-

tate God, without any lingering sin or decay. The voice from
the throne depicts the cessation of tears, death, and decay,
and declares, "It is done! I am the Alpha and the Omega, the
beginning and the end. To the thirsty I will give from the
spring of the water of life without payment. The one who
conquers will have this heritage, and I will be his God *and
he will be my son*.[17] But as for the cowardly, the faithless, the
detestable, as for murderers, the sexually immoral, sorcerers,
idolaters, and all liars, their portion will be in the lake that
burns with fire and sulfur, which is the second death" (Rev.
21:6–8 ESV). The contrast between what God's son experi-
ences and how all the rest behave establishes the perfection of
this sonship. The use of sonship to refer to our consummated
resurrection-existence surfaces also in Paul (Rom. 8:23: "We
wait eagerly for our adoption to sonship, the redemption of
our bodies").

(7) The major New Testament writers find ways to distinguish between Jesus's sonship and the sonship of believers. In
John's Gospel, only Jesus is referred to as ὁ υἱός ("the son")
of God; believers are characteristically referred to as τὰ τέκνα
or τὰ παιδία ("the children") of God (e.g., John 1:12). In
Paul, although υἱός can be used to refer to both Jesus and to
the believer, only believers are sometimes described as being
sons *by adoption* (Rom. 8:15, 23; 9:4; Gal. 4:5; Eph. 1:4–5).
Adoption to sonship can refer to God's choice of Israel as his
covenant people (Rom. 9:4), to the reality that true believers
under the terms of the new covenant are sons of God (in the

---

[17] This is the ESV rendering; the NIV reads: "Those who are victorious will inherit all this,
and I will be their God *and they will be my children*." The loss of the son metaphor in this
context is regrettable, for while "children" maintains the image of family relationship, it
does not so powerfully depict imitation and identity.

fourth sense, above; Rom. 8:15; Gal. 4:5; Eph. 1:4–5), and to the consummated sonship we shall enjoy in resurrection existence (in line with the sixth sense, above; Rom. 8:23).

THE USE OF "SON OF GOD" TO REFER TO JESUS

In this final section we shall survey the ways in which "Son of God" is applied to Jesus. Doubtless other analyses are possible. Here my purpose is merely to identify distinguishable christological uses. In the next chapter I shall try to unpack something of the theology that undergirds these distinctive uses.

(1) This first category is the catchall.[18] In it are the many references in which Jesus is asserted to be, or assumed to be, the Son of God. Excluded are most references where "Son of God" is clearly tied to one or more of several important themes—Davidic Messiah, for example—that are treated below.

The range is enormous. A partial list includes the following. The angel tells Mary, "The Holy Spirit will come on you, and the power of the Most High will overshadow you. So the holy one to be born will be called the Son of God" (Luke 1:35). When the disciples witness Jesus's power in the stilling of the storm, after his walking on the water, they exclaim, "Truly you are the Son of God" (Matt. 14:33). The voice of God speaks at the transfiguration, excluding Moses and Elijah and promoting Jesus: "This is my Son, whom I love; with him I am well pleased. Listen to him!" (Matt. 17:5; see Mark 9:7; Luke 9:35). The Father is determined that "all

---

[18]For simplicity, I will not include passages where Jesus is referred to as ὁ παῖς, which some older versions rendered "son" instead of "servant" (Matt. 12:18; Luke 2:45; Acts 3:13, 26; 4:27, 30).

may honor the Son just as they honor the Father" (John 5:23), and the Father is glorified through the Son (John 14:13). "Whoever believes in the Son has eternal life, but whoever rejects the Son will not see life, for God's wrath remains on them" (John 3:36). After the resurrection it is customary to preach that Jesus is the Son of God (Acts 9:20). After Jesus's ascension, believers sometimes simply refer to him as the Son of God (e.g., "These are the words of the Son of God, whose eyes are like blazing fire . . ." Rev. 2:18), even as they "wait for [God's] Son from heaven, whom he raised from the dead" (1 Thess. 1:10). Paul preaches the gospel of God's Son (Rom. 1:9); sinners are reconciled to God by the death of God's Son (Rom. 5:10). Those whom God foreknows he predestines to be conformed to the image of his Son (Rom. 8:29)—the Son he did not spare, in a gift that is the final measure of God's gracious largesse (Rom. 8:32). Indeed, the measure of God's faithfulness is that he has called his people "into fellowship with his Son, Jesus Christ our Lord" (1 Cor. 1:9). God sent his Son "that we might receive adoption to sonship," and then sends the Spirit of his Son into our hearts—the Spirit who calls out, "*Abba*, Father" (Gal. 4:4–6). In all of this, God "has rescued us from the dominion of darkness and brought us into the kingdom of the Son he loves, in whom we have redemption, the forgiveness of sins" (Col. 1:13–14). "And our fellowship is with the Father and with his Son, Jesus Christ" (1 John 1:3). In that fellowship, we also have "fellowship with one another, and the blood of Jesus, [God's] Son, purifies us from all sin" (1 John 1:7). The Son is the climax of all antecedent revelation (Heb. 1:2). "God has given us eternal life, and this life is in his Son" (1 John 5:11). In some remarkable passages, Jesus's sonship is tied to his calling as Great High Priest (Heb. 4:14; 7:28).[19]

(2) My second category of christological uses embraces those passages in which "Son" or "Son of God" is linked to Jesus's role as the promised Davidic king. The foundational text is 2 Samuel 7:13–14, even though, as we have seen, when God says, "I will establish the throne of his kingdom forever. I will be his father, and he will be my son," the person initially in view is Solomon. When Solomon does wrong, God will punish him with temporal judgments. God adds, "But my love will never be taken away from him, as I took it away from Saul, whom I removed from before you" (7:15). Saul could not even be said to establish a dynasty. His line on the throne lasted only as long as his own life. David knew full well that either he or his heirs would fall into gross evil and idolatry that would disqualify them from reigning over those who were in fact *God's* people under *God's* reign; apart from the intervention of God, David's line would end like Saul's. But grace will triumph, God avers: those in David's line would face no more than temporal judgments, so that the dynasty would endure. Then comes this final word of the oracle: "Your house and your kingdom will endure forever before me; your throne will be established forever" (2 Sam. 7:16). Although the text does not raise the options, this surely means, if the promise is not empty rhetoric, that either the Davidic dynasty will be forever perpetuated by an endless string of successors, or that the Davidic dynasty will be forever perpetuated when someone in David's line eventually arises who reigns forever.

---

[19] Beale, *A New Testament Biblical Theology*, esp. 400–429, is inclined to see more frequent connections than I do between these various Son of God passages and Adam as the primal son of God. He is invariably thought-provoking and may be right.

A string of Old Testament promises fleshes out and further specifies this Davidic anticipation. I shall mention only two. God's promise to David took place about 1000 BC. In the eighth century BC, in words we still recite every Christmas, the prophet Isaiah announced, "For to us a child is born, to us a *son* is given, and the government will be on his shoulders" (Isa. 9:6). But this is no ordinary Davidide: "Of the greatness of his government and peace there will be no end. He will reign on David's throne and over his kingdom, establishing and upholding it with justice and righteousness from that time on and forever. The zeal of the LORD Almighty will accomplish this" (9:7). More: "And he will be called Wonderful Counselor, Mighty God, Everlasting Father, Prince of Peace" (9:6). Toward the beginning of the sixth century BC, the word of the Lord comes through the prophet Ezekiel, declaring that the Lord himself will be the shepherd of his people. The point is repeated about twenty-five times with powerful rhetorical effect ("I will rescue my flock. . . . I myself will search for my sheep. . . . I will bring them out from the nations. . . . I will pasture them on the mountains of Israel. . . . I will tend them. . . . I myself will tend my sheep and have them lie down . . . " Ezek. 34:10–15). Yet the oracle ends with the Lord declaring, "I will place over them one shepherd, my servant David, and he will tend them; he will tend them and be their shepherd. I the LORD will be their God, and my servant David will be prince among them. I the LORD have spoken" (34:23–24). The visitation of the Lord and the coming of his servant David become more than a little blended. Other Old Testament passages further develop these themes (e.g., Psalm 2; 89:27).

Thus the Davidic king, sometimes referred to as God's "anointed" (Ps. 2:2) or "Messiah" and hence "Christ" from the Greek (a title about which I shall say more in chapter 2), is God's Son, and he is to rule as God rules, to imitate God in this respect—indeed, in some passages, like Isaiah 9:6, he is identified with God. Before she gives birth to Jesus, Mary is told by the angel Gabriel, "He will be great and will be called the Son of the Most High. The Lord God will give him the throne of his father David, and he will reign over Jacob's descendants forever; his kingdom will never end" (Luke 1:32–33). When Nathanael first meets Jesus, he declares, "Rabbi, you are the Son of God; you are the king of Israel" (John 1:49), thus again tying together sonship and Davidic kingship.[20] The purpose of his Gospel, John tells us, is "that you may believe that Jesus is the Messiah, the Son of God, and that by believing you may have life in his name" (John 20:31).[21] Peter's famous confession at Caesarea Philippi reads (in Matthew's presentation), "You are the Messiah, the Son of the living God" (Matt. 16:16). Paul begins his longest letter by introducing "the gospel [God] promised beforehand through his prophets in the Holy Scriptures regarding his Son, who as to his earthly life was a descendant of David, and who through the Spirit of holiness was appointed the Son of God

---

[20] Even where "Son of God" is not used, numerous passages make it clear that the kingdom of God or the kingdom of heaven that Jesus preaches (Matt. 4:17) is equally *his* kingdom. For example, in the explanation of the parable of the weeds, we are told that the Son of Man "will send out his angels, and they will weed out of *his* kingdom everything that causes sin and all who do evil" (Matt. 13:41), while "the righteous will shine like the sun *in the kingdom of their Father*" (13:43). Cf. Matt. 25:31, 34, 40.

[21] I have argued at length elsewhere that this verse is better translated "that you may believe that the Messiah, the Son of God, is Jesus"—thus providing a more forceful identification that indicates the *known* category is the Messiah, the Son of God. Cf. D. A. Carson, "The Purpose of the Fourth Gospel: John 20:31 Reconsidered," *Journal of Biblical Literature* 108 (1987): 639–51; Carson, "Syntactical and Text-Critical Observations on John 20:30–31: One More Round on the Purpose of the Fourth Gospel," *Journal of Biblical Literature* 124 (2005): 693–714.

in power by his resurrection from the dead: Jesus Christ our Lord" (Rom. 1:2–4). Sometimes Jesus's sonship is specifically connected with his kingdom, his reign: for example, God "has rescued us from the dominion of darkness and brought us into the kingdom of the Son he loves" (Col. 1:13). At other times Jesus's sonship is tied to his title Messiah or Christ: he is the anointed King. Thus in John's first letter, the two confessions of the truth, each repeated twice, are: (1) the Messiah is Jesus (1 John 2:22; 5:1), the denial of which amounts to the denial of the Father and the Son (1 John 1:22–23); (2) the Son of God is Jesus (1 John 4:15; 5:5). No reader can forget that the opening line of the New Testament announces "the genealogy of Jesus the Messiah the son of David" (Matt. 1:1), which, if the trajectory from 2 Samuel 7:14 on is taken into account, makes him the Son of God.

(3) In some christological uses of "Son of God," there is another overtone lurking nearby. At Jesus's baptism, the voice from heaven says, "This is my Son, whom I love; with him I am well pleased" (Matt. 3:17). Many commentators rightly observe that the first part of the quotation calls to mind Psalm 2, where the messianic king is God's Son; the second part calls to mind Isaiah 52:13–53:12, which portrays the Suffering Servant. In Matthew's ordering of the narrative, however, Jesus is then immediately led by the Spirit into the wilderness to be tempted (Matt. 4:1–11). As part of that temptation, Satan twice taunts Jesus with the words, "If you are *the Son of God*" (Matt. 4:3, 6), designed to call to mind God's words at Jesus's baptism, words that presuppose his messianic, kingly, calling. But Jesus defends himself in all three temptations with words from the Old Testament that

clearly refer to Israel as a whole (Deut. 8:3; Ps. 91:11, 12; Deut. 6:13), not to Israel's king. And as we have seen, sonship language is sometimes applied in the Old Testament to Israel collectively, or to Israelites taken individually or together. In other words, Satan tempts Jesus as the Son of God, the King of Israel, but Jesus defends himself as should any Israelite, as should Israel as a whole, without actually using the word "son" in this way. This is in line with a well-recognized theme in Matthew: this Gospel likes to present Jesus as in some sense the ultimate Israel, the true Israel. Jesus recapitulates something of Israel's experience when he, too, is called out of Egypt, and the words "Out of Egypt I called my son" are applied to him (Hos. 11:1; Matt. 2:15).[22]

(4) Perhaps the most stunning christological sonship passages, however, are those that assign transparently divine status to the Son, or speak, with varying degrees of clarity, of his preexistence. Some of the texts we have already canvassed have leaned in this direction, of course—as when the Father determines that all should honor the Son just as they honor the Father (John 5:23). Yet we should reflect on a handful of other passages. In the past, the writer to the Hebrews avers, God spoke to the Fathers through the prophets, but now in these last days he has given us the Son-revelation—the Son "whom he appointed heir of all things, and through whom also he made the universe. The Son is the radiance of God's glory and the exact representation of his being, sustaining all things by his powerful word" (Heb. 1:2–3). The Word

---

[22] On this quotation, see the important essay by G. K. Beale, "The Use of Hosea 11:1 in Matthew 2:15: One More Time," forthcoming. I am grateful to Dr. Beale for showing me a draft of his essay. Cf. D. A. Carson, "Matthew," in *Matthew–Mark*, Expositor's Bible Commentary 9 (2nd ed.; Grand Rapids, MI: Zondervan, 2010), 118–20.

that was with God in the beginning (and thus God's own fellow) and was God (and thus God's own self) "became flesh and made his dwelling among us. We have seen his glory, the glory of the one and only Son, who came from the Father, full of grace and truth" (John 1:1, 14). It is not that this eternal Word *became* the Son by means of the incarnation, so that it is appropriate to speak of Father, Son, and Holy Spirit only *after* the incarnation, whereas *before* the incarnation it would be more appropriate to speak of the Father, the Word, and the Spirit. No, for as we have seen in Hebrews, *the Son* is the one by whom God made the universe. In John 3:17, we are told, "God did not send *his Son* into the world to condemn the world, but to save the world through him." It is fanciful to suppose this means that God sent into the world someone who became the Son after he arrived. "The Son is the image of the invisible God, the firstborn over all creation. . . . He is before all things, and in him all things hold together. . . . For God was pleased to have all his fullness dwell in him"; indeed, "all things have been created through him and for him" (Col. 1:15–19), making him not only God's agent in creation but creation's master and goal. In these and numerous other passages (e.g., Matt. 11:27; Luke 10:22; John 14:9; 17:1–8; 1 John 5:20), Jesus is not the Son of God by virtue of being the ultimate Israel, nor is he the Son of God by virtue of being the Messiah, the ultimate Davidic king, nor is he the Son of God by virtue of being a perfect human being. Rather, he is the Son of God from eternity, simultaneously distinguishable from his heavenly Father yet one with him, the perfect Revealer of the living God.

It is time to wrap this up. The biblical material on Son of

God, let alone on the diversity of son metaphors, is extremely rich. I have not listed all the evidence, though I have tried to summarize all the *kinds* of evidence. Nor have I mentioned the handful of passages in which ambiguity regarding the meaning of "Son of God" may well be intended by the human author, such as Mark 15:39 (= Matt. 27:54), where the centurion witnesses Jesus's death and cries, "Surely this man was the Son of God." But we have set ourselves up for more probing explorations of a small number of passages and themes.

Chapter Two

"SON OF GOD" IN
SELECT PASSAGES

If this were a major study on "Son of God" as a christological title, the next step would be a detailed exegetical study, book by book and corpus by corpus, of all the occurrences of the title—or at least of well-chosen representatives of all the occurrences. Instead, in this chapter I shall direct my attention primarily to two extended passages, Hebrews 1 and John 5:16–30. The aim in both cases is to understand what the New Testament writers meant when they declared Jesus to be the Son of God, at least in these passages, and how they reached that decision by their reading of the Old Testament Scriptures they loved. I have chosen these two passages because they seem to me to be among the richest and most evocative of biblical passages to treat this title. In neither case, however, will I offer a phrase-by-phrase reading of the entire unit. That would make for a very long chapter. Rather, I shall pick and choose details in each passage, treating some at length while skipping by others and merely dropping hints. On the other hand, I shall feel free to draw in biblical texts and themes from outside the two primary passages I have selected, if by so doing we better perceive the sweep of biblical witness and move toward a theological synthesis in which the whole is even more compelling than the parts.

HEBREWS 1

It will prove helpful to develop the argument by asking and answering six questions.

Why Is the Son Greater Than the Angels?

That is the claim made by Hebrews 1:4: the Son "became as much superior to the angels as the name he has inherited is superior to theirs." The justification of this claim is developed in the following verses. The first step is taken in verse 5: "For to which of the angels did God ever say, 'You are my Son; today I have become your Father'? Or again, 'I will be his Father, and he will be my Son'?"

The superiority that is claimed does not turn on the mere word "Son," as if the text were saying, "Jesus is called the Son, but angels are not so described in Scripture, so that proves Jesus is superior." Anyone as well-versed in Scripture as the writer to the Hebrews cannot possibly be ignorant of the fact that sometimes Scripture *does* refer to angels as sons of God, as we saw in chapter 1. The comparison must turn on more than the mere word "Son." This observation drives us to try to determine why the author thinks the two Old Testament texts he quotes, Psalm 2:7 and 2 Samuel 7:14, prove the superiority of the Son over angels, when angels are not mentioned in either text.

The problem becomes more acute when we recall that the first of the two quotations, Psalm 2:7, is cited three times in the New Testament, and on each occurrence taken to prove something different. Here it is taken to prove that Jesus is superior to angels. In Hebrews 5:5 the author appeals to the same verse to prove that Jesus did not take on himself the glory of becoming a high priest. After all, when Aaron became high priest under the terms of the old covenant, he did not take this honor on himself, but rather was appointed by God (5:4), so when under the terms of the new covenant Jesus becomes high priest, he similarly has to be appointed by God. This appointment, the writer to the Hebrews insists, is demonstrated by the quotation from Psalm 2:7: "You are my Son; today I have become your Father." The third and final occurrence of this quotation is found in Acts 13, in Paul's evangelistic address in the synagogue in Pisidian Antioch. Paul introduces the quotation with the words, "What God promised our ancestors he has fulfilled for us, their children, by raising up Jesus.[1] As it is written in the second Psalm: 'You are my son; today I have become your father'" (Acts 13:32–33).

In short, New Testament texts quote Psalm 2:7 to prove Jesus is superior to angels, to prove Jesus did not take on himself the glory of becoming high priest but was appointed by God, and to demonstrate that God has fulfilled his promises to the Israelite ancestors by raising Jesus from the dead—even though, on the face of it, Psalm 2 does not mention angels, has no interest in the high priest's office, and makes no mention of the resurrection of the Messiah.

Thus we are driven to the second question.

---

[1] The context shows that what Paul means by this "raising up Jesus" is raising up Jesus from the dead.

How Are Psalm 2:7 and 2 Samuel 7:14 Relevant?

We begin by reminding ourselves of what we have already observed in 2 Samuel 7:14. There, we saw, God promises to build a "house" for David, that is, a household, a dynasty. Whenever a new scion of David's line comes to the throne, at that point he becomes God's "son"—that is, God has "generated" him by bringing him to this role, and the king himself pledges to reign as God reigns, and to reign under God, with justice, integrity, and covenantal faithfulness. But suppose one of David's descendants becomes notoriously evil? Will not God then destroy David's line, as he destroyed King Saul, the first monarch of the united monarchy? No, he will not. To accomplish his promise to give David a perpetual dynasty, God promises not to punish David or any of his descendants with more than temporal punishments. The promise of an eternal dynastic line is unqualified: "Your house and your kingdom will endure forever before me; your throne will be established forever" (2 Sam. 7:16).

That is the background to Psalm 2. It is possible to read this psalm, in the first instance, against the historical background of the Davidic kings in the first half of the first millennium BC. The surrounding small nations, over which the throne of David ruled during the reigns of David and Solomon, might well conspire against the Davidic overlord. "The kings of the earth," as they are called (2:2), might be understood to be "kings of the land": the Hebrew could be rendered that way. But any rebellion against, say, King David, is no less a rebellion against the Lord who stands behind David—and who could ever stand against him? "The One enthroned in heaven laughs; the Lord scoffs at them" (2:4). Note that the Lord is *enthroned*: his is the ultimate throne behind the Davidic throne, and he is the King behind the king. It is he who has appointed David; it is he who has anointed David. The rebellion is "against the LORD and against his anointed" (2:2)— that is, against YHWH and his Messiah,[2] the Davidic king. The Lord is, we might say, the father-king, while David is the son-king. In his wrath the Lord thunders, "I have installed my king on Zion, my holy mountain" (2:6).

At this point the Davidic king speaks: "I will proclaim the LORD's decree: He said to me, 'You are my son; today I have become your father'" (Ps. 2:7), thus utilizing exactly the same son imagery that is found in 2 Samuel 7:14. God continues to address his son, his appointed Davidic king: "Ask me, and I will make the nations your inheritance, the ends of the earth your possession" (2:8). Once again, the Hebrew might just about allow us to understand "tribes" instead of "nations," and "land" instead of "earth." Similarly in verses 10–11: "Therefore, you kings, be wise; be warned, you rulers of the earth [land?]. Serve the LORD with fear and celebrate his rule with trembling." Nevertheless, the extravagance of the promise, combined with little hints like "ends of the earth" ("ends of the land" does not quite cut it), points to a Davidic monarch who outstrips both David and Solomon, not to mention all their heirs and descendants down to the exile. The tight-

---

[2] It is widely recognized that "anointed" (usually transliterated "messiah" from the Hebrew and "christ" from the Greek) is commonly applied in the Old Testament to kings and priests, since literal anointing accompanied the appointment to the office in both cases. More rarely a prophet was anointed and so might be designated "messiah." In other words, there is nothing *intrinsically* forward-looking about the term itself—or, to put it more provocatively, there is nothing in "messiah" that is *intrinsically* messianic. Nevertheless, that assessment changes as soon as one discerns the trajectories, the typologies, of kingship and priesthood that *do* race forward to an anticipated climax. Read canonically, "messiah" becomes messianic, in exactly the same way that 2 Samuel 7:14 and Psalm 2:7, read canonically, anticipate the ultimate Davidic king.

ness of the relationship between the Lord and his son-king is wonderfully explicit when verse 11 and verse 12 are read together: "Serve the LORD with fear. . . . Kiss his son,[3] or he will be angry and your way will lead to your destruction, for his wrath can flare up in a moment." Conversely: "Blessed are all who take refuge in him" (2:12).

In short, both 2 Samuel 7:14 and Psalm 2:7 depict the Davidic monarch as God's son, ideally imitating his heavenly father's kingly rule. Both passages hint at a Davidic reign that eclipses anything in the first millennium BC. Both are elements in a trajectory of anticipatory passages that run through the Old Testament—passages, as we saw in chapter 1, like Isaiah 9, which looks forward to a son/king in David's line whose government is eternal and who is described as the Mighty God and the Everlasting Father,[4] and like Ezekiel 34, where YHWH comes to shepherd his sheep, apparently in the person of the Davidic king whom he sends. Old Testament writers say so many more things of this anticipated Davidic king. He establishes worldwide rule (Pss. 18:43–45; 45:17; 72:8–11; 89:25; 110:5–6) that is marked by morality and righteousness (Ps. 72:7) and utter faithfulness to the Lord (Ps. 72:5). He is preeminent among men (Ps. 45:2, 7), the friend of the poor and the enemy of the oppressor (Ps. 72:2–4, 12–14). He is the heir of the covenant with David (Pss. 89:28–37; 132:11, 12)

---

[3] The nest of translation challenges in this verse, not least surrounding the rendering "son," does not really affect the central point. The Semitic word used is the Aramaic *bar* rather than the Hebrew *ben* (both words mean "son"), but the absence of the article prompts some to think the word should really be read as Hebrew *bōr* (the vowels were not part of the original), taken adverbially ("kiss sincerely" or "kiss purely"). Other suggestions have been offered. These suggestions make little difference for our purposes, since the word "son" has already been used unambiguously in the decree (2:7), thus linking this passage to 2 Samuel 7:14, and connecting the appointment of the human king, under the heavenly king, with the engendering of the son.

[4] Perichoresis eight centuries before Christ?

and of Melchizedek's priesthood (Ps. 110:4). He belongs to
the Lord (Ps. 89:18) and is utterly faithful to him (Pss. 21:1,
7; 63:1–8, 11). He is, as we have seen, YHWH's son (Pss. 2:7;
89:27), seated at his right hand (110:1).

This trajectory—or, to use the more traditional terminology, this Davidic typology—is inherently forward-looking. It
anticipates that toward which it points. *When Hebrews 1:5
quotes Psalm 2:7 with reference to Jesus, it is the Davidic
typology that warrants it*; that is, the writer to the Hebrews
is reading Psalm 2:7 not as an individual prooftext but as one
passage within the matrix of the Davidic typology it helps
to establish. That he is thinking in terms of this trajectory,
this typology, is clear from the fact that he immediately links
Psalm 2:7 with 2 Samuel 7:14, not to mention Psalm 45:6–7
(quoted in Heb. 1:8–9) and Psalm 110 (quoted in Heb. 1:13).
In other words, Jesus is superior to the angels in his role as
long-anticipated Davidic king, long-anticipated Messiah,
long-anticipated Son of God. As the son/king, Jesus brings in
the kingdom; angels could not do that.

But When Does the Kingdom Dawn?

In one sense, of course, God's kingdom, or, better, his reign,
is universal and inescapable: "his kingdom rules over all" (Ps.
103:19). With that sense of kingdom in view, which is coextensive with his sovereignty, we are all in it—Christian, Muslim,
Hindu, atheist alike. Yet in the Old Testament, God reigns in
a peculiar and redemptive way over the Israelites, and thus,
via his appointed Davidide, over the Davidic kingdom. As
anticipation mounted for the coming of the ultimate Davidic
king, it was recognized that that kingdom, when it dawned,

would be redemptive and transformative. Now that Christ has risen from the dead and is seated at the Father's right hand, both these senses of "kingdom," the universal and the redemptive, persist. On the one hand, all authority is given to Christ in heaven and on earth (Matt. 28:18). All of God's sovereignty is now mediated through Christ (1 Cor. 15:24–28). In that sense, Christ's kingdom is inescapable. On the other hand, Christ's kingdom is regularly conceived of as that subset of his total reign under which there is transformed, eternal life. We cannot see or enter this kingdom apart from the new birth (John 3:3, 5). This kingdom is already in operation, permeating this lost world the way yeast permeates a lump of dough (Matt. 13:33). It is the supreme treasure to be pursued (Matt. 13:44–46). And at its consummation, every knee will bow and every tongue confess that Jesus is Lord, to the glory of God the Father (Phil. 2:9–11).

So assuming the redemptive and transformative sense of kingdom, this saving sense, when does the kingdom dawn?

One might say that it dawned with the birth of the King. "Where is the one who has been born king of the Jews?" the Magi asked. "We saw his star when it rose and have come to worship him" (Matt. 2:2). Jesus was not born merely to inherit the kingdom; it was his by right, his by birth.

In another sense, we might argue that Jesus's kingdom dawns with the onset of his public ministry. His baptism at the hands of John the Baptist declares him to be the Son whom God loves (primarily denoting the Davidic king) and the Suffering Servant. Immediately after his temptation, he begins to preach in Galilee, in fulfillment of the prophecy of Isaiah 9 to the effect that a light has dawned in Galilee of the Gentiles (Matt. 4:15–16)—and it is in this context that Jesus preaches, "Repent, for *the kingdom of heaven* has come near" (Matt. 4:17).

Some might prefer to think the onset of the kingdom takes place in connection with the training of the seventy (or seventy-two), when Jesus's disciples return with rejoicing that even the demons submit to them in Jesus's name. Jesus responds by saying that in their ministry he saw Satan fall like lightning from heaven (Luke 10:17–18).

Others may recall how Matthew plays with the theme of Jesus reigning from the cross (Matt. 27:27–51a). It is not only a matter of the *titulus*, "This is Jesus, the King of the Jews" (27:37), but the mockery of soldiers ("Hail, king of the Jews!" 27:29) and of the religious authorities ("He's the king of Israel! Let him come down now from the cross, and we will believe in him," 27:42), not to mention the sovereign way in which he gives up his spirit (27:50)—an authoritative, kingly act. Granted the frequency of the "king" references in Matthew 27, it is hard to deny that, whatever the centurion and those with him meant when, thoroughly terrified, they exclaimed, "Surely he was the Son of God!" (27:54), for Matthew and his readers this sonship signaled, at very least, messianic kingly status in David's line.

But doubtless the event most connected with the dawning of the kingdom is Jesus's resurrection. It is in the wake of the resurrection that Jesus insists that all authority has been given to him (Matt. 28:18). The two disciples on the Emmaus road had hoped that Jesus "was the one who was going to redeem Israel" (Luke 24:21), that is, they hoped he was the long-awaited Davidic king. In this expectation, however,

they had no category for a crucified Davidic king, a crucified Messiah. Jesus rebukes their folly and asks, "Did not the
Messiah have to suffer these things and then enter his glory?"
(24:26). This, he insists with a larger group of disciples, is
what is written: "The Messiah will suffer and rise from the
dead on the third day" (v. 46). In other words the Messiah,
the Davidic king, has come into his own, and thus, implicitly,
his kingdom has dawned. We have already observed that in
John's Gospel the message to which the disciples bear witness,
the message that is to be believed if eternal life is to be gained,
is that the Messiah, the Son of God, is Jesus (John 20:30–31),
and this message is trumpeted in the wake of Jesus's resurrection appearances. We have also observed how Paul links the
resurrection of Jesus to the onset of Jesus's mediatorial reign
(1 Corinthians 15).

The kingdom of God in its uncontested form, of course,
does not come until the end of the age. Until then we pray
as the Lord taught us: "Your kingdom come, your will be
done, on earth as it is in heaven" (Matt. 6:10). That is why
inheriting the kingdom can on occasion be envisaged as an
entirely *future* event (e.g., 1 Cor. 6:9–10). This consummation, however, when Jesus hands over the kingdom to God
the Father (1 Cor. 15:24), is irrefragably bound up with the
general resurrection, *of which Jesus's resurrection is the first-
fruits* (1 Cor. 15:20), thus showing once again how central
the resurrection of Jesus is for the dawning of the kingdom,
for the coming of the king. Moreover, just as the kingdom
of God sometimes refers to the entire sweep of God's reign,
and sometimes to that subset of his reign under which there is
salvation for his own people, so also Jesus's reign can embrace

all of God's sovereignty, all authority in heaven and on earth (Matt. 28:18), and sometimes can refer to that subset of his reign under which there is life (e.g., 1 Cor. 6:9–10). These reflections shed some light on why, in Acts 13:33– 34, Paul connects Psalm 2 with Jesus's resurrection. In Paul's mind, the divine decree that declares, "You are my son; today I have become your father" (Ps. 2:7), thus appointing as king the ultimate David in the Davidic trajectory, takes place most dramatically and irrefutably in Jesus's resurrection. From now on he reigns with all authority, in anticipation of the glorious consummation.

Is the Davidic King God?

As the writer to the Hebrews continues to argue for the superiority of the Son over the angels, he writes:

> But about the Son he says,
>
> "Your throne, O God, will last for ever and ever;
>   a scepter of justice will be the scepter of your
>   kingdom.
> You have loved righteousness and hated wickedness;
>   therefore God, your God, has set you above your
>   companions
>   by anointing you with the oil of joy." (Heb. 1:8–9)

The words are quoted from Psalm 45:6–7. To understand the passage both in its original context in Psalm 45 and in Hebrews 1, we must reflect on at least four details.

(1) The flow of the passage. The superscription asserts Psalm 45 to be a wedding song, which, as we shall see, makes eminent sense. The first verse is the writer's reflec-

tion on what he is doing as he pens the psalm (not unlike other psalm introductions: see 37:1–3; 49:1–4): "My heart is stirred by a noble theme as I recite my verses for the king; my tongue is the pen of a skillful writer" (45:1). This introduction casts the writer as a courtier of some sort, and the one who is getting married is the king. The next verses affirm the king's majesty and moral stature (45:2–5). Not a few of the lines sound a tad hyperbolic if applied to most of the Davidic kings we know from the Old Testament: "You are the most excellent of men. . . . In your majesty ride forth victoriously in the cause of truth, humility and justice; let your right hand achieve awesome deeds" (45:2, 4). The following verses (45:6–9) include the lines quoted in Hebrews 1. The courtier addresses the king as he might address God: "Your throne, O God, will last for ever and ever; a scepter of justice will be the scepter of your kingdom. You love righteousness and hate wickedness" (45:6–7). A similar thought is found in Psalm 89:14: "Righteousness and justice are the foundation of your throne"—but there the person addressed is God himself. At least it is clear in Psalm 45 that the mandate of this king is to rule with the integrity and righteousness that God displays in his rule. But make no mistake: the courtier is still addressing the Davidic king. It is not as if he has suddenly turned to God and so is no longer speaking to the human king. That is made clear in verse 7: because this human king rules in righteousness, "therefore God, your God, has set you above your companions by anointing you with the oil of joy" (45:7). Clearly, then, there is a God, designated "your God," above the king who is addressed as God, who has been anointed. The ensuing verses address the bride (45:10–12) and describe

the wedding procession (45:13–15). The closing verses are
again addressed to the king (45:16–17).

(2) This pair of closing verses demands special attention. The fruit of this marriage is progeny: that is the way it
is supposed to be in a royal wedding that seeks heirs for the
throne: "Your sons will take the place of your fathers; you
will make them princes throughout the land" (45:16). This
demonstrates that the king whose wedding this is must be an
ordinary Davidide before the coming of Jesus. No one takes
the place of Jesus; no one succeeds him on the throne. So in
the first instance, the psalm cannot legitimately be allegorized
into the wedding between Christ and his people or the like.
This wedding anticipates heirs who are successors, displacing
their fathers. That means it is an ordinary Davidic king who
is addressed as God.

(3) In Psalm 45 the courtier, presumably one of the sons
of Korah, addresses the Davidic king; in Hebrews 1, it is God
himself who addresses the king, who is clearly Jesus. Granted
the strength of the Davidic typology, it is not surprising that
a passage focusing on a Davidic figure can equally be applied
to the ultimate Davidic figure. On further reflection, the
shift from the courtier addressing the Davidic figure to God
himself addressing the Davidic figure is not all that hard to
understand either. The common assumption is that Scripture
is, finally, God's communication. If God sanctions this form
of address to a Davidic king on the lips of a courtier, then
precisely because this is God's communication, the courtier's
categories are God's categories: God himself addresses the
Davidic king as God.

(4) We must not overlook the fact that the quotation in

Hebrews 1 is introduced by the words, "But *about the Son* he [God] says" (1:8). That reminds the reader that the appointment of any Davidide to the throne is equivalent to making him *the son of God*, in language stemming from 2 Samuel 7:14 and Psalm 2, the focal verses quoted in Hebrews 1:5. And as in 2 Samuel 7, so also in Psalm 45: the immediate referent is *necessarily* a Davidic king *other* than Jesus—and yet these texts are nestled within a Davidic trajectory that can be fulfilled *only* in Jesus.

So the question to puzzle over in Psalm 45 is this: How can the courtier address the king, who because of the last verses of the psalm, *must* not be Jesus, as God? The difficulty is so patent that numerous alternative translations have been offered: "God is your throne" or "Your throne is [a throne of] God, eternal" or the like.[5] But after examining five different proposals, Murray Harris demonstrates that the traditional reading is not merely easily defensible, but the most obvious and satisfactory of the options.[6] Moreover, as strange as the expression is when applied to a pre-Jesus Davidic king, it is not entirely unparalleled. God tells Moses, "See, I have made you God to Pharaoh" (Ex. 7:1 AT),[7] which of course does not mean that God thinks Moses has become indifferentiable from God himself. The point is that Moses's ruling authority in the relevant matters is the ruling authority of God. So

---

[5] E.g., cf. the RSV: "Your divine throne endures forever and ever."

[6] Murray J. Harris, "The Translation of *Elohim* in Psalm 45:7–8," *Tyndale Bulletin* 35 (1984): 65–89. See also H. W. Bateman, "Psalm 45:6–7 and Its Christological Contributions to Hebrews," *Trinity Journal* 22 (2001): 3–21. See the slight update in Bateman's book *Jesus as God: The New Testament Use of* Theos *in Reference to Jesus* (Grand Rapids, MI: Baker, 1992), chs. 8 (187–204) and 9 (205–27).

[7] Both the NIV and the ESV render the Hebrew, "See, I have made you like God to Pharaoh." In fact, every major modern English translation opts for "like God," "as God," or "seem like God," all of which renderings are, contextually speaking, semantically accurate and happily orthodox, but entirely lacking in the rhetorical punch of the original.

also in Psalm 45: the courtier does not think the king he is addressing is literally, ontologically, God, as verse 7 makes clear.[8] The psalm is loaded with hyperbolic expressions of the king's majesty, integrity, justice, humility, and power, precisely because these were the standards the king was *supposed* to maintain if he, *as the son of God*, was tasked with reigning as his Father reigns.

When we turn to the quotation in Hebrews, once again some scholars prefer alternative renderings: "God is your throne," or "Your throne is God," taking ὁ θεός as either the subject or a predicate nominative, respectively. But there are very good reasons for taking the expression as a vocative:[9] the Son is addressed, "Your throne, O God, will last for ever and ever." But is this quotation in Hebrews 1 as hyperbolic as it is in Psalm 45? That brings us to the fifth question.

Is the Son of God in Hebrews 1 Any Greater Than David and His Immediate Heirs and Successors?

One might, I suppose, begin to answer this question by observing how consistently the New Testament portrays Jesus as outstripping all who came before him. In Hebrews the "Jesus is better" theme[10] shines especially brightly: Jesus is better than the angels (Hebrews 1); Jesus is better than Moses (Heb. 3:5–6); Jesus is better than Joshua (Heb. 4:8–10); Jesus is better than Aaron (Hebrews 7); Jesus's priest-

---

[8] See the discussion in Peter T. O'Brien, *The Letter to the Hebrews*, The Pillar New Testament Commentary (Grand Rapids, MI: Eerdmans, 2010), 72–75.

[9] See especially Murray J. Harris, "The Translation and Significance of ὁ θεός in Hebrews 1:8–9," *Tyndale Bulletin* 36 (1985): 129–62.

[10] The word "better" (κρείττων) appears thirteen times in Hebrews, as against nineteen for the entire New Testament. All thirteen serve "to contrast Christ and the new order with what went before him" (O'Brien, *Hebrews*, 61).

hood is better than the Levitical priesthood (Hebrews 7); the covenant of which he is the mediator is better than the old covenant (Hebrews 8); his sacrifice is better than the sacrifices of *Yom Kippur* (Hebrews 9–10); the heavenly sanctuary into which he enters is better than the earthly sanctuary (Heb. 9:1–10); his blood is better than the blood of bulls and goats (Heb. 9:14); and so forth. One might also recall the question Jesus poses to his interlocutors: "What do you think about the Messiah? Whose son is he?" (Matt. 22:41–46; Mark 12:35–37; Luke 20:41–44). They rightly understand the Messiah to be the kingly, Davidic Messiah, and insist that the correct answer is "the son of David." But Jesus insists that David addresses his future heir as "Lord" (citing Ps. 110:1), and in that culture no father would ever address his son as "Lord": the respect and veneration should run from the son to the father, not the other way round. "Son of David" may be a true description of Jesus, but it is also inadequate. He is every bit as much "Son of God" as David himself was—and, unavoidably, he must be *greater* than David for David to think of him in this way.

In fact, we need not pursue all these paths to answer our question, for the immediate context, the first chapter of Hebrews, answers it for us. The opening verses of Hebrews 1 constitute a prologue to the book (1:1–4). Here the Son-revelation outstrips all previous revelation. Moreover, this Son is not only the God-appointed heir of all things (that is, the Davidic king *par excellence*, the owner and ruler of everything), but also God's own agent in the creation of the entire universe, "the radiance of God's glory and the exact representation of his being," the one who even now reigns over all by his powerful word, the one who "provided purification for sins," the one who is already seated "at the right hand of the Majesty in heaven."[11] The prologue concludes: "So he became as much superior to the angels as the name he has inherited is superior to theirs" (1:4)—apparently drawing a stunning contrast: in eternity past he already had the name that made him superior to the angels (After all, who created whom?), but at some point *became* superior to them *again*, by dying a death for the purification of sins and then being so vindicated that he sat down at God's right hand.[12] *Thus the sonship language applied to Christ in the prologue cannot be restricted to a strictly Davidic-messianic horizon.* The writer to the Hebrews, in other words, is prepared to link, within his first chapter, Jesus's sonship in the Davidic, messianic sense, with his sonship in the sense of his thoroughly divine status, embracing his preexistence and his oneness with God in creation. Because those themes have been established in Hebrews 1 before Psalm 45 is quoted, it is virtually impossible not to see that when God addresses the Son with the words, "Your throne, O God, will last for ever and ever," the words "O God" cannot be taken hyperbolically as they could with David

---

[11] See Richard Bauckham, *Jesus and the God of Israel* (Grand Rapids, MI: Eerdmans, 2008), esp. ch. 7, "The Divinity of Jesus in the Letter to the Hebrews" (233–53).

[12] It would take us too far afield to explore in detail why the writer to the Hebrews chooses to contrast Christ with angels. At least part of the answer is bound up with the fact that angels were understood to have mediated the law given to Moses (Acts 7:38–39; Gal. 3:19; Heb. 2:2; see Ex. 3:2; 12:23; Isa. 63:9). Much of Hebrews is devoted to showing that the law of Moses was *not* the final step in God's plan of redemption, but one of the steps that pointed forward to Christ. To establish Jesus's superiority over the angels, both in eternity past as their Creator and this side of the resurrection as their Lord, establishes their rightful place. At the same time, the incarnation establishes this Son of God as the redeemer of fallen human beings, not of fallen angels (Hebrews 2). See the discussion in O'Brien, *Hebrews*, 61–63; and in Richard Bauckham, "Monotheism and Christology in Hebrews 1," in *Early Christianity in Context*, eds. L. T. Stuckenbruck and W. E. S. North (London: T&T Clark, 2004), 167–85.

and his immediate heirs. This Son, quite simply, is to be thought of as God.[13]

To return again, then, to the quotation of Psalm 2:7 in Hebrews 1:5, Jesus is superior to the angels not only because Old Testament texts and their trajectories point to him as the long-promised Davidic king whose rule extends to the whole world and brings in the consummation, but also because he is not *just* David's heir and thus the Son of God by virtue of being the Davidic king, but he is *also* the Son of God by virtue of his preexistence and unqualified divine status. No angel can match him on either score.

That brings us to the sixth and final question.

But How Does Any of This Argumentation Bear on Jesus's Priestly Status, So Important in Hebrews 5:5?

Here we note that the last Old Testament quotation in Hebrews 1 is from Psalm 110: "To which of the angels did God ever say, 'Sit at my right hand until I make your enemies a footstool for your feet'?" (Heb. 1:13). This part of Psalm 110 establishes the messianic, Davidic king in much the way that Psalm 2 does. It establishes Jesus's superiority over the angels for exactly the same reasons that Psalm 2 offers. But readers of Hebrews will recall that Psalm 110, much quoted in this book, includes a second oracle: "The LORD has sworn and will not change his mind: 'You [still addressed to the messianic king] are a priest forever, in the order of Melchizedek" (Ps. 110:4). That theme is developed in hugely important and

---

[13] Bauckham, *Jesus and the God of Israel*, 241–44, arrives at this conclusion for Hebrews 1:5–14, but without working through what the cited texts meant in their original contexts, that is, without teasing out the logic of the trajectories that *warrants* the exegesis of the author of Hebrews.

complex ways in Hebrews 7. For our purposes it is enough to observe that the same Lord who promises total victory over enemies to the messianic king also swears that this king will be a priest forever. And in truth, Jesus enters into his high priestly role in the light of, in the wake of, his death and resurrection. It appears, then, that applying Psalm 2:7, "You are my son; today I have become your father," to the Father's commitment to establish Jesus as high priest, is not so far removed from this matrix of texts after all.

Part of our problem is that we have been influenced by a certain strand of contemporary scholarship that envisages christological themes in atomistic ways. Over here is a Son of Man christology; over there is a Son of God christology dependent on Davidic monarchy; yet again, in another place, there is a high priestly christology; and so forth. But were there any Christians in the first century who claimed, "Frankly, I'm a 'Son of Man' christology Christian; I don't go in for this high priestly stuff," or "I must say I thoroughly believe in the messianic 'Son of God' christology, and I can put up with the Suffering Servant themes, but I can't quite get myself to believe in a preexistent 'Son of God' christology." Judging by the evidence of Hebrews 1—and a treatise could be written to demonstrate similar support through much of the New Testament—Christians commonly plugged away at *integrating* confessional christologies. Just as we discovered, in chapter 1, that Matthew can leap from an Israel-as-Son-of-God christology to a Davidic-king-as-Son-of-God christology, showing no embarrassment at affirming that Jesus is the Son of God in both senses, so Hebrews 1 leaps from preexistent-Godhead-as-Son-of-God christology to Davidic-king-Messiah-as-Son-of-God christology.

The writer so integrates his argument that the defining strands of the complementary christologies have been woven into one organic whole, so that it is neither advisable nor even possible to try to pull them apart. The coherence of the argument of the chapter forbids it. Only then do we truly see how the trajectory from Psalm 2:7, "You are my son; today I have become your father," simultaneously establishes Jesus's superiority to the angels, finds its "today" in the resurrection of Jesus and the dawning of his kingdom, and establishes Jesus, by God's will, as high priest in the order of Melchizedek. And that is why Psalm 2:7 is quoted in Hebrews 1:5; 5:5; and Acts 13:33–34. What holds this reasoning together is in no small part the web of allusive uses of "Son" and "Son of God."

JOHN 5:16–30

Although this passage demands at least equal time, I shall provide only the most cursory survey.[14]

The Setting for a Discourse on Sonship

The immediate setting is Jesus's miraculous healing of the man who had been paralyzed for thirty-eight years. "Get up!" Jesus told him. "Pick up your mat and walk" (John 5:8). The man did so, presumably to head home. John tells us this took place on the Sabbath, so the man was stopped by the authorities for carrying a burden on the Sabbath day (5:10).

---

[14] See D. A. Carson, *The Gospel according to John*, Pillar New Testament Commentary (Grand Rapids, MI: Eerdmans, 1991), 246–59.

The man blamed Jesus for telling him to carry the mat, and this in turn led to his disclosure that Jesus had healed him on the Sabbath.

"So, because Jesus was doing *these things* [presumably both healing and instructing the man to carry his mat] on the Sabbath, the Jewish leaders began to persecute him" (5:16). Doubtless at this juncture Jesus might have interacted with the Jewish leaders at the level of typical *halakhic* controversy—that is, he might have entered into sharp dialogue with them over what the law actually stipulates, over what the obedience to the law actually looks like. He might have said, "Come on! You can't be serious! It's not as if I'm a medical professional trying to make a little extra money on the Sabbath by opening the doors to my surgery when they should be closed. Prohibition of work on the Sabbath did not have in view the performance of a miracle in order to release from paralysis a son of Israel! And so what if this man was carrying his mat home! It's not as if he was a professional mat-carrier trying to fill his pocket with a few extra shekels instead of observing the Sabbath. Your interpretations of the law are indefensible." If Jesus had responded along those lines, there would have been a sharp debate, but no persecution, and certainly no attempt to kill him. After all, various Jewish parties were actually engaged in such *halakhic* debates.

To understand the explosive significance of what Jesus *actually* said, it is helpful to remember that at the time there were ongoing religious debates as to whether God himself kept the law. The point where controversy erupted was the Sabbath. If God rested on the Sabbath, some argued, then wouldn't the entire universe become disordered every seventh day? Must not God keep up his work of providential rule? So surely God does *not* keep the Sabbath. The other side pointed out that the codification of Sabbath law into thirty-nine categories of prohibited work established that you could carry a burden *within* your domicile, but never from one domicile to another, and that even within your domicile, you could never hoist a burden up onto your shoulder—it could never be that heavy. But since the entire universe is God's, he never moves any part of it to another domicile; and since he is bigger than all of it, and moves things around by his powerful word, he never has to hoist heavy burdens onto his shoulders. So even if God continues to reign providentially on the Sabbath, he is not, strictly speaking, breaching Sabbath law.

Whether it is exactly this debate that was percolating in the background in Jesus's day, or something like it, the point is that both sides were saying, in effect, that God continues to "work" in some sense, but ended up debating whether or not it really counted as work. Into some such a situation as this, Jesus defends himself by saying, "My Father is always at his work to this very day, and I too am working" (5:17). This utterance establishes at least three things. *First,* by referring to God as "my Father," Jesus is implicitly saying that he himself is God's Son. *Second,* because in the context Jesus is arguing that he has the right to do things on the Sabbath that other human beings do *not* have the right to do, he is declaring his sonship to be unique. *Third,* because the warrant for Jesus's work on the Sabbath is grounded in the fact that God, his Father, works on the Sabbath, Jesus is implicitly claiming he has the prerogatives of God.

Small wonder that we read, "For this reason they tried all the more to kill him; not only was he breaking the Sabbath, but he was even calling God his own Father, making himself equal with God" (5:18). Jews, after all, saw themselves as "sons of God" in some sense, but they rightly perceive that Jesus is claiming something more than that by his references to God as his Father. If he is claiming that he must be held at the same level as God, enjoying God's prerogatives (which, from the perspective of the Jewish leaders, was unthinkable), he is a blasphemer. Nevertheless, it is crucial to grasp that what the Jewish leaders mean by "equal with God" is not quite what Jesus means. They envisage some kind of ditheism, in which there are two gods, the Father and Jesus, more or less parallel and equal to each other. Such a stance utterly vitiates monotheism; small wonder they are appalled. But that is not what Jesus has in mind. In the following verses Jesus provides a defense of his utterance, of his claim that he is God's Son, that he has the prerogatives of God. In other words, Jesus is taking some steps toward the articulation of what would become the peculiarly Christian form of monotheism.

Argument for a Peculiar Kind of Sonship
We may analyze the argument in three steps:

(1) The Son insists he is subordinate to the Father, but it is a uniquely defined subordination (John 5:19–23). "Very truly I tell you, the Son can do nothing by himself; he can do only what he sees his Father doing" (v. 19). In other words,

Jesus the Son of God does not constitute a second God-center. John's Gospel repeatedly affirms Jesus's deity (1:1; 8:58; 14:9; 20:28). Nevertheless, this passage underscores the Son's functional subordination, and it is not the only one to do so. In addition to this verse, recall 5:30 ("By myself I can do nothing; I judge only as I hear, and my judgment is just, for I seek not to please myself but him who sent me"), 8:29 ("The one who sent me is with me; he has not left me alone, for I always do what pleases him"), and 14:31 (the prince of this world attacks Jesus, he explains, "so that the world may learn that I love the Father and do exactly what my Father has commanded me"). In other words, one way of avoiding the reprehensible notion of two gods is by insisting that the Son is in some sense subordinate to his Father.[15]

Yet what a uniquely defined subordination it is. Jesus's claim to functional subordination in 5:19 is followed by four "for" (γάρ) statements in the original.

(a) *For* "whatever the Father does the Son also does" (5:19b). We have witnessed how the father/son imagery is often tied up with the maxim "Like father, like son." For example, because God is the supreme peacemaker, the person who makes peace may be called a son of God (Matt. 5:9). But Jesus claims that *whatever* the Father does, he does. His imitation of the Father is exhaustive. You and I could not possibly make such a claim. For a start, we have not created a universe—but this Son has (John 1:1–3). Moreover, although there are many hints in verses 19–30

---

[15] Obviously this exegesis has relevance to the contemporary debates about equality and functional subordination and their relevance both to patristic understanding of the Godhead (about which I will say a little more in the next chapter) and to ongoing disputes over egalitarianism and complementarianism (about which I will say nothing more).

that it is the incarnate Son who is in view, this passage must include activities (like the creation) that took place in this Son's preincarnate existence. You and I cannot claim pre-existence. In short, Jesus grounds his functional subordination to the Father in his claim to *coextensive* action with his Father—and transparently, that makes his sonship unique. And necessarily, it also raises a raft of ontological questions not here addressed.

(b) *For* "the Father loves the Son and shows him all he does" (5:20). In John's Gospel, because the Father loves the Son, he has placed everything in the Son's hands (3:35); the Father loved the Son before the creation of the world (17:24); here, the Father loves the Son and shows him all he does, thus (in the flow of the argument) making it possible for the Son to do all that the Father does. Elsewhere we are told that the Son loves the Father, and in consequence the Son perfectly obeys the Father (14:31). In other words, their love for each other is perfectly reciprocated, but the way it works out maintains a subtle functional distinction. The Father is never said to obey the Son, and the Son does not show the Father what he is doing so as to authorize the Father to do likewise. But the important thing to note for our purposes is the force of the initial "For": this circle of love *explains* verse 19: it is *because* of the Father's love for the Son that the Son can do everything the Father does.[16] Indeed (the argument continues), the Father

---

[16] It would take us too far away from the argument to tease out two further points, but they should at least be noted. (1) The marvelous self-disclosure of the Father in the Son turns, in the first place, *not* on God's love for us, but on his love for his Son. Similarly, the Son's redemptive work turns, in the first place, not on the Son's love for us but on his love for his Father, and consequently on his obedient willingness to go to the cross. The world must indeed learn that the Son loves his Father and always does what pleases him. (2) This perfect circle of love is precisely what guarantees the perfection of the Son-revelation. On the one side is the perfection of the Father's love that "shows" the Son everything; on the other side is the perfection of the Son's love that perfectly accomplishes the Father's will

will show the Son greater things yet (v. 20b): here the incarnate Son is in view, and this "showing" guarantees that the Son will complete his mission, namely, all that the Father has given him to do—which leads to:

(c) *For* "just as the Father raises the dead and gives them life, even so the Son gives life to whom he is pleased to give it" (5:21). In other words, this γάρ ("for") introduces the supreme exemplification of the fact that the Father has more to "show" the Son. God alone has power to raise people from the dead, and because he has "shown" this to the Son, the Son has this power no less than the Father.

(d) *For*[17] in this case the Father has determined not to keep final judgment in his own hands but to delegate it to his Son, to entrust it to his Son (5:22), "that all may honor the Son just as they honor the Father. Whoever does not honor the Son does not honor the Father, who sent him" (5:23). But this does not mean that the Son who now exercises all final judgment strikes out on his own. After all, in the last verse of this paragraph, Jesus insists, "I judge only as I hear, and my judgment is just, for I seek not to please myself but him who sent me" (5:30).[18]

In short, the Son insists he is subordinate to the Father, but it is a uniquely defined subordination.

(2) The Son insists that, like the Father, he has life-in-

---

and performs all that the Father does. See D. A. Carson, *The Difficult Doctrine of the Love of God* (Wheaton, IL: Crossway, 2000); Carson, "Love and the Supremacy of Christ in a Postmodern World," in *The Supremacy of Christ in a Postmodern World*, eds. John Piper and Justin Taylor (Wheaton, IL: Crossway, 2007), 85–89.

[17] Once again the Greek provides γάρ, which the NIV renders as "Moreover" (which loses the logical flow) and the ESV, rather strangely, omits entirely.

[18] To continue an analogy from the first chapter, it is as if Stradivarius Senior entrusts the making and application of the varnish to Stradivarius Junior: henceforth that will be his domain. But that does not mean that Stradivarius Junior gets uppity and decides to experiment with his own varnish; he joyfully follows his father's will.

himself. The Son, Jesus asserts, has the authority and power to grant people eternal life now, and will raise the dead to resurrection life on the last day (5:24–25). The reason he has such power is explained in verse 26: "For as the Father has life in himself, so he has granted the Son also to have life in himself." On first reading, this verse is very strange. To say that the Father has life in himself is to say he is self-existent; his life depends on no other. We might capture this by inserting hyphens and affirming that the Father has life-in-himself. But what can it possibly mean to say that he has *granted* the Son also to have *life-in-himself*? If the Father has *granted* the Son life, that would make sense of the verb "granted," but then of course the Son would be ontologically inferior to the Father: he would not be God, for although he would have life, it would be derived life and not life-in-himself. If the text affirmed, "Just as the Father has life-in-himself, so the Son has life-in-himself," that would affirm that both Father and Son are equally God, but it would be almost impossible to escape the charge of ditheism. But how are we to understand that the life-in-himself Father has *granted* the Son to have life-in-himself?

The proffered explanations, like certain courses of demons, are legion, but I suspect the best explanation is an old one: this is an eternal grant. It is not a grant given to Jesus at some point in time, as if *before* that point he did *not* have life-in-himself. After all, John has already insisted that the pre-incarnate Word had life in himself (1:4). Thus John 5:26 helps to establish the peculiar relationships between the Father and the Son, in eternity and from eternity. It is an eternal grant.

(3) The Son of God insists he is also the Son of Man, and as such, he is the Father-sanctioned judge of all. The Father has given the Son "authority to judge because he is the Son of Man" (5:27). In other words, the Father has entrusted all judgment to the Son not only because he loves him and wants all to honor the Son even as they honor the Father (5:22–23), but also because the Son of God is also the Son of Man. This is the only place in the Gospels where "Son of Man" is anarthrous; almost certainly this has the effect of reducing the titular force of the expression. In other words, it is not the well-known figure of Daniel 7 who is most likely in view, but the sentence means something like this: The Father has given the Son authority to judge because he is a human being. God's justice is inevitably perfect, but by entrusting final judgment to the Son, the Father has placed it in the hands of the one member of the Godhead who is as much human as he is God. This does not change the outcome of the judgment (after all, as we have seen, the Son's judgment is perfectly aligned with his Father's will, 5:30), but it ensures that we human beings have additional reason to grasp that our judgment is in the hands of the Word who became flesh, who was, as Hebrews puts it, tempted in all points as we are, yet never succumbed to sin.

Here, then, is Jesus's explanation to the Jewish leaders of his peculiar sonship. He does not back away one millimeter from his claim that he has all the prerogatives of God, that he does all that his Father does, that he is to be revered as his Father is revered. And yet he makes his claim with arguments that carefully avoid giving any impression that he is a separate God-center, a second but equal God. Although his language is largely functional, it is simply impossible to over-look the ontology that is presupposed behind it.[19] Here, in short, are some of the exegetical pieces that would be forged into what would one day be called Trinitarianism.

And that takes us to the last chapter.

---

[19] Bauckham, *Jesus and the God of Israel*, 235, prefers to avoid the paired alternatives of functional christology and ontological christology in favor of "divine identity." In the end, however, he cannot entirely escape them: "A Christology of divine identity thus offers a way beyond the misleading alternatives of functional Christology or ontological Christology. Certain divine 'functions', if we have to use that word, are not mere functions, but integral to who God is. If Jesus performs such functions and if monotheism is to be retained, as it was in early Christianity, then he must belong to the identity of the one God. Jesus cannot function as God without being God. The point becomes even clearer once we recognize that a clearly ontological condition attaches to the divine functions of creation and sovereign rule. Only the one who alone is eternal in the full sense can be the Creator of all things and sovereign Ruler of all things. When this uniquely divine eternity is attributed also to Jesus, it is clear that the early Christians knew precisely what they were doing in Jewish theological terms, when they understood Jesus to participate in the creative work and the eschatological rule of the one God." Exactly.

CHAPTER THREE

"JESUS THE SON OF GOD" IN CHRISTIAN AND MUSLIM CONTEXTS

In an ideal world, we should attempt a great deal more exegesis and careful integration to develop a comprehensive theology of "Son of God" as a christological title. Only then should we venture forth on wide-ranging reflections on the confessional, pastoral, and translational significance of what we have uncovered so far. But since this is not an ideal world, it may be worth plunging ahead somewhat prematurely. At very least this may have the advantage of priming the pump of discussion.

I shall organize this last chapter under two questions.

WHAT BEARING DOES THIS STUDY OF JESUS AS THE SON OF GOD HAVE ON THE WAY CHRISTIANS SHOULD THINK ABOUT JESUS?

I shall focus on six items.

1. Not All Uses of "Son of God" Are the Same

Owing not least to the Trinitarian confessionalism that we have inherited from the fourth century, "Son of God" as a christological confession is in many Christian minds primarily associated with the second person of the Godhead. It has become a fixed datum. This is not so much wrong as too narrowly focused—or, better put, some New Testament passages use Son of God terminology to ascribe to Jesus the attributes that were so important in third- and fourth-century christological debates, but many New Testament passages use Son of God terminology in rather different ways. Sometimes it functions much as it did when it referred to Israel as God's Son, only now, in effect, Jesus is the ultimate Israel. Sometimes "Son of God" is associated with Jesus's status as the anointed Davidic king, the Messiah, with particular emphasis on his kingly authority. Sometimes the expression focuses on his earthly ministry; sometimes it presupposes his origins in eternity past.

In short, in the New Testament "Son of God" is not a *terminus technicus*, as the Latins say—a technical term that always carries the same associations. It always presupposes some sense of deriving from God, or of acting like God, or both, but the domains of such acting are pretty diverse. Bible readers should exercise special pains not to succumb either to unjustified reductionism, in which one particular usage is read into every occurrence, or to "illegitimate totality transfer," in which the entire semantic range of the expression is read into every occurrence. Context must decide.

2. Biblical Trajectories Are Important If We Are to Understand How "Son of God" Commonly "Works"

This should not surprise us. In various ways, New Testament writers are constantly drawing lines between, on the one hand, Old Testament persons, institutions, and events, and, on the other hand, Jesus. Thus Jesus is the true Manna, the bread from heaven; he is the Passover Lamb; he is the True Vine; when he is "lifted up" to die, this recalls the lifting up of the serpent in the wilderness; he is the ultimate High Priest; he himself is the Temple of God. So it should not come as a surprise that Jesus is declared to be the ultimate Davidic King, and thus the Son of God (as each Davidic king was declared Son of God in turn).

Yet this Davidic trajectory is subtle. We have observed how 2 Samuel 7:14, Psalm 2:7, and Psalm 45:6–7 are applied to Jesus, even though the first certainly applies to Solomon, not Jesus, the second probably applies first of all to David and his immediate successors, and the third certainly applies, initially, to kings who had heirs who replaced their fathers, not to Jesus. Yet in all three cases the context drops hints of a fulfillment that outstrips local petty monarchs. Once these passages are nestled into the complex matrix of the Davidic typology, the many passages that anticipate an heir of David who is declared to be God and whose reign embraces the entire earth and even the heavens, the connection to Jesus is all but inevitable. If these trajectories are not identified and understood, however, we will be at a loss to understand how the Old Testament texts that are said to be fulfilled in Jesus actually "work." Many is the Christian who has thumbed through Old Testament pages to find the passage that has been quoted by the New Testament and applied to Jesus, only to feel let down by the fact that the connection is at best obscure, and in some cases seems to be talking about something radically different. It takes some hard work to uncover how these trajectories, these typologies, actually work. But when we take the time and effort to examine them, we are hushed in awe at the wisdom of God in weaving together intricate patterns that are simultaneously so well hidden in their development and so magnificently obvious in their fulfillment.

3. The Relationship Between the Exegesis of the Biblical "Son of God" Passages and the Categories of Systematic Theology Is Not a Simple One
There are several domains to this problem, of which I shall mention three. *First*, the ways in which both exegesis and systematic theology are commonly taught ensure that the two disciplines do not engage each other very well. Of course, there are wonderful exceptions. Nevertheless, it is rare for commentaries and courses in biblical exegesis to carry the argument forward all the way to the categories and integration demanded by systematic theology. More commonly, those who teach exegesis warn against imposing the categories of systematic theology onto the biblical texts. Reciprocating in kind, many a systematician teaches theology with minimal dependence on firsthand study of the biblical texts. In fact, contemporary systematic theology frequently generates dissertations on, say, John Owen's view of the atonement (which properly belongs to historical theology) or perichoresis and personhood in the Trinity (which largely turns on philosophical theology), with relatively little work devoted to the kind of constructive, normative theology that builds a case, starting from the Bible, of what Christians *ought* to believe. Moreover, systematicians are sometimes at least as disdainful of rigorous exegesis as biblical scholars are of systematic theology.

Second, the words used in the two disciplines commonly have rather different meanings. It is as if some of the same vocabulary is being deployed in two rather different domains of discourse. The example I commonly offer is "sanctification." This side of the Reformation, it is common for systematicians to teach us that, while justification refers to that once-for-all act of God by which he declares sinners to be just, not on the basis of their own righteousness but on the basis of Christ's righteousness and atoning death, sanctification is that ongoing process by which believers are becoming more holy. All recognize that there are instances when the sanctification word-group refers not to the process of becoming more holy but to the status of a person: someone has been set aside for God, and in that sense "sanctified." That status may be every bit as instantaneously received and as once-for-all as justification. Justification lies in the domain of the forensic; sanctification lies in the domain of the religious and the sacred. Time has taught us to think of such occurrences of the "sanctification" word-group as positional or definitional sanctification. Some biblical experts strongly argue that *most* occurrences of the word sanctification in the New Testament are actually instances of such positional sanctification.[1]

Systematicians in turn may start to wonder if the doctrine of sanctification is being stripped away from them by the biblical experts. Meanwhile, one cannot help but observe how Paul can speak yearningly of the goals he maintains: "to know Christ—yes, to know the power of his resurrection and participation in his sufferings, becoming like him in his death, and so, somehow, attaining to the resurrection

---

[1] See esp. David Peterson, *Possessed by God: A New Testament Theology of Sanctification and Holiness* (Leicester, UK: IVP, 1995).

from the dead" (Phil. 3:10–11). Indeed, he has not arrived at his goal, but presses on "to take hold of that for which Christ Jesus took hold of me" (Phil. 3:12). All of this sounds very much like sanctification even though the word "sanctification" is not used. In short, sometimes when we have "sanctification," we do not have sanctification, and sometimes where there is no "sanctification" there is plenty of sanctification. In short, the doctrine and the word-group are not tightly tied together. Too few biblical scholars and systematicians show us how to establish the doctrine from the Scriptures—the former because they are inclined to think it is not their job, and the latter because they think the confessional standard has already been established and does not need rearticulation.

Third, to make matters more complicated, systematic theology often develops its own specialist terminology not found in the Bible. Such terminology may be the fruit of centuries of theological reflection on what the Bible says, but once it gains traction it takes on a life of its own. One need go no farther than the word "Trinity." Systematicians may view the doctrine of the Trinity as so well established that they need not lay the foundations again; biblical scholars may view the doctrine as a fourth-century development and therefore outside the purview of their own specialism. Almost as bad, the doctrine of the Trinity may be reduced to a simple formula: for example, "The Father is God, the Son is God, the Spirit is God, and there is but one God." That is true, of course, and so the formula may then be justified by a handful of attendant and relevant proof-texts. But all of this short-circuits how the doctrine of the Trinity came to avoid the Arian christology, with its lesser-god view of Jesus; the modalism of Sabellius, with the one God disclosing himself in three manifestations that could not actually interact with one another as persons; the Nestorian understanding that emphasizes the differences and disunity between the divine and human natures of Jesus; and adoptionism that teaches Jesus was born a human being and only later became the Son of God. Pretty soon the doctrine of the Trinity was surrounded by expressions like "essence," "substance," "person," and "hypostatic union"—none of which is controlled by Old Testament and New Testament usage. Yet all of these debates and their attendant specialty vocabulary arose from close readings of the New Testament and from attempts to avoid *mis*reading the biblical evidence. One recalls John Calvin's elegant discussion of the doctrine of the Trinity, and then his conclusion: "Say that in the one essence of God there is a trinity of persons: you will say in one word what Scripture says, and cut short empty talkativeness." Those who "persistently quarrel" over these words, he avers, "nurse a secret poison."[2] Rightly deployed, confessional standards ought to guide, shape, and enrich our exegesis; wrongly deployed, they become cut off from the biblical texts that nurtured and developed them.

It is easy to see how these reflections on the tension between exegesis and systematic theology have a bearing on our understanding of what it means, as Christians, to confess that Jesus is the Son of God. In most seminaries there is not a clear educational track that helps students move easily and intelligently from how the Bible uses "Son of God" to the Trinitarian use of the title to which all of us are grateful heirs.

---

[2] John Calvin, *Institutes of the Christian Religion*, ed. John T. McNeill, trans. Ford Lewis Battles (Philadelphia: Westminster, 1960), 1.13.5.

The danger, on the one hand, is succumbing to the mindless biblicism that interprets texts, and translates them, without wrestling with the syntheses that actually preserve biblical fidelity, and, on the other hand, relying on confessional formulas while no longer being able to explain in some detail how they emerge from reflection on what the Bible actually says. Although chapters 1 and 2 were the merest introductions to the recovery of the exegetical and theological work that needs to be undertaken in every generation, they stand, I hope, as pointers in the right direction.

4. The "Eternal Generation of the Son" Is Especially Convoluted Territory

It is important to remember what this formula was trying to preserve. As important as it is to defend the deity of the Son in some sonship passages, not least against both the antisupernaturalism of much of the Western world and the anti-Trinitarian monotheism of the Muslim world, it is equally important to preserve the biblical emphasis on the truth of monotheism: there is but one God. To affirm that the Father is God and the Son is God and the Spirit is God, without unpacking the relationships among them, is perpetually in danger of succumbing to tritheism. Leaving aside for our purposes the relationship between the Holy Spirit and the Father and the Son, and focusing exclusively on the Father/Son relationships, the eternal generation of the Son became the standard way of avoiding multiple gods. To illustrate how the eternal generation of the Son has been handled in influential systematic theology, I shall quote at length from Berkhof:

The eternal generation of the Son. The personal property of the Son is that He is eternally begotten of the Father (briefly called "filiation"), and shares with the Father in the spiration of the Spirit. The doctrine of the generation of the Son is suggested by the Biblical representation of the first and second persons of the Trinity as standing in the relation of Father and Son to each other. Not only do the names "Father" and "Son" suggest the generation of the latter by the former, but the Son is also repeatedly called "the only-begotten," John 1:14, 18; 3:16, 18; Heb. 11:17; 1 John 4:9. Several particulars deserve emphasis in connection with the generation of the Son: (1) *It is a necessary act of God.* Origen, one of the very first to speak of the generation of the Son, regarded it as an act dependent on the Father's will and therefore free. Others at various times expressed the same opinion. But it was clearly seen by Athanasius and others that a generation dependent on the optional will of the Father would make the existence of the Son contingent and thus rob Him of His deity. Then the Son would not be equal to and *homoousios* [of the same essence] with the Father, for the Father exists necessarily, and cannot be conceived of as non-existent. The generation of the Son must be regarded as a necessary and perfectly natural act of God. This does not mean that it is not related to the Father's will in any sense of the word. It is an act of the Father's necessary will, which merely means that His concomitant will takes perfect delight in it. (2) *It is an eternal act of the Father.* This naturally follows from the preceding. If the generation of the Son is a necessary act of the Father, so that it is impossible to conceive of Him as not generating, it naturally shares in the eternity of the Father. This does not mean, however, that it is an act that was completed in the far distant past, but rather that it is a timeless act, the act of an eternal present, an act always continuing and yet ever completed. Its eternity follows not only from the eternity of God, but also from the divine immutability and from the true deity of the Son. In addition to this it can be inferred from all those passages of Scripture which teach either the pre-existence of the Son or His equality with the Father, Mic. 5:2; John 1:14, 18; 3:16; 5:17, 18, 30, 36; Acts 13:33; John 17:5; Col. 1:16; Heb. 1:3. The statement of Ps. 2:7, "Thou art my Son; this day have I begotten thee," is generally quoted to prove the generation of the Son, but, according to some, with rather doubtful propriety, cf. Acts 13:33; Heb. 1:5. They surmise that these words refer to the raising up of Jesus as Messianic King, and to the recognition of Him as Son of God in an official sense, and should probably be linked with the promise found in II Sam. 7:14, just as they are in Heb. 1:5. (3) *It is a generation of the personal subsistence rather than of the divine essence of the Son.* Some have spoken as if the Father generated the essence of the Son, but this is equivalent to saying that He generated His own essence, for the essence of both the Father and the Son is exactly the same. It is better to say that the Father generates the personal subsistence of the Son, but thereby also communicates to Him the divine essence in its entirety. But in doing this we should guard against the idea that the Father first generated a second person, and then communicated the divine essence to this person, for that would lead to the conclusion that the Son was not generated out of the divine essence, but created out of nothing. In the work of generation there was a communication of essence; it was one indivisible act. And in virtue of this communication the Son also has life in Himself. This is in agreement with the statement of Jesus, "For as the Father hath life in Himself, even so gave He to the Son also to have life in Himself," John 5:26. (4) *It is a generation that must be conceived of as spiritual and divine.* In opposition to the Arians, who insisted that the generation of the Son necessarily implied separation or division in the divine Being, the Church Fathers stressed the fact that this generation must not be conceived in a physical and creaturely way, but should be regarded as spiritual and divine, excluding all idea of division or change. It brings *distinctio* and *distributio*, but no *diversitas* and *divisio* in the divine Being. (Bavinck) The most striking analogy of it is found in man's thinking and speaking, and the Bible itself seems to point to this, when it speaks of the Son as the Logos. (5) The following definition may be given of the generation of the Son: *It is that eternal and necessary act of the first person in the Trinity, whereby He, within the divine Being, is the ground of a second personal subsistence like His own, and puts this second person in possession of the whole divine essence, without any division, alienation, or change.*[3]

Observe several details.

(a) Berkhof links the eternal generation of the Son with the expression "only-begotten," which he says is regularly predicated of the Son, adducing as evidence John 1:14, 18; 3:16, 18; Hebrews 11:17; and 1 John 4:9. The Greek word is μονογενής. The rendering "only-begotten" presupposes it derives from μόνος + γεννάω. But a very good case can be made for a derivation from μόνος + γένος, and hence "only one of its kind," which has generated the modern translations "only" (ESV) and "one and only" (NIV). Berkhof's list of proof-texts is not reassuring: one of the six, Hebrews 11:17, does not refer to Jesus at all, but describes Isaac as Abraham's μονογενής son—certainly not Abraham's "only-begotten" son, nor even his "only" son, but properly his unique son, in

---

[3] Louis Berkhof, *Systematic Theology* (Grand Rapids, MI: Eerdmans, 1949), 93–94.

that sense his one and only son. In a private communication, Gerald Bray has pointed out that toward the end of the second century, Tertullian in his *Adversus Praxean* talks about the *filius unicus*, the unique Son, which demonstrates how he at least read μονογενής.

(b) Another comment by Berkhof betrays an unease with the standard proof-texts for the eternal generation of the Son: "The statement of Ps. 2:7, 'Thou art my Son; this day have I begotten thee,' is generally quoted to prove the generation of the Son, but, according to some, with rather doubtful propriety, cf. Acts 13:33; Heb. 1:5. They surmise that these words refer to the raising up of Jesus as Messianic King, and to the recognition of Him as Son of God in an official sense, and should probably be linked with the promise found in II Sam. 7:14, just as they are in Heb. 1:5." This sounds as if Berkhof has not quite decided on which side to come down. I would like to think that my exegesis in chapter 2 might help him decide.

(c) The complex stipulations Berkhof advances doubtless could be shown to arise out of some biblical descriptions of the Son, but he does not take the time to make the demonstration. The result is a feeling that the discussion has slipped away from the world of unyielding biblical texts.

(d) In any case, I tried to show, in chapter 2, that the relationship between the Father and the Son, commonly enfolded in the "eternal generation of the Son," is better anchored in the broad themes of a passage like John 5:16–30, rising to its apex in 5:26, where the Father who has life-in-himself grants to the Son to have life-in-himself, than in a questionable rendering of μονογενής.

5. *Understanding Jesus as the Son of God Ought
to Have a Bearing on Our Evangelism*

In past generations—how far back depends on the location—
our evangelism in the Western world was largely confined to
the churchified and to those who had at least been exposed to
basic Christian doctrine. To insist on the importance of believing on Jesus the Son of God, or to preach that God sent his
Son into the world to save the world, raised few eyebrows: the
"Son" language was so much a part of the heritage that very
little was done to unpack it. Today, however, in much of the
Western world, we are dealing with biblical illiterates. What
does it mean to them when they hear that God has a Son, or
that God sent his Son into the world to bear our sins in his
own body on the tree? This is not a subtle-but-wicked plea to
avoid complex doctrines. Far from it: rather, just as we have
to start farther back in our evangelism to provide more of the
Bible's story line for the good news of Jesus to cohere—much
as Paul provides much of the Bible's story line when he preaches
the gospel to biblically illiterate pagans (Acts 17:16–31)—so we
have to unpack more of the doctrine of God, and thus of the
Son, to a generation that knows nothing of the Trinity. There
are many ways of doing this, of course, but one of them is to follow the biblical trajectories forward, unpacking the Son of God
themes as we go, until we reach their climax in Jesus the Son
of God—the true man, the true Israel, the true Davidic King,
the one who comes as David's Son and yet as the mighty God.

6. *Understanding Jesus as the Son of God Ought
to Have a Bearing on Our Worship*

We increase the intensity, joy, and fidelity of our worship,
not by including the verb "to worship" in every second line in

our so-called "worship songs," but by knowing more about God, and bringing our adoration to him, as he is. Insofar as our conceptions of him diverge from what he has disclosed of himself, so far are we worshiping a false god, which is normally called idolatry. To study hard what holy Scripture says about the Son of God, who has most comprehensively revealed his heavenly Father, is to know more about God, and thus to begin to ground our worship in reality rather than slogans.

WHAT BEARING DOES THIS STUDY OF JESUS AS THE SON OF GOD HAVE ON CURRENT DEBATES REGARDING THE TRANSLATION OF THE TITLE, ESPECIALLY IN MUSLIM CONTEXTS?

The issues have become embroiled in much larger issues that deserve discussion. I shall merely identify them before moving on.

C5 and IM

An article appeared in 1998 titled "The C1 to C6 Spectrum: A Practical Tool for Defining Six Types of 'Christ-Centered Communities.'"[4] The author was John Travis, a pseudonym for a husband/wife team that had been living and serving for twenty years in a tightly knit Asian Muslim community. The "C" component came from "Christ-Centered Communities" in the title. The C1 to C6 categories are:

C1: A traditional church using nonindigenous language. Its believers exist in the broader community as an ethnic/

---

[4] *John Travis*, titled "The C1 to C6 Spectrum: A Practical Tool for Defining Six Types of 'Christ-Centered Communities,'" *Evangelical Missions Quarterly* 34 (1998): 407–8.

religious minority, regularly viewed by the local population as essentially foreign. One might imagine, say, English-language churches in Japan. In Muslim cultures that permit them, such churches are largely cut off from the surrounding culture, although a few Muslim-background believers may be found in them.

C2: Here the church is akin to C1, but the indigenous language is used. The vocabulary, forms of corporate worship, and other cultural values are essentially foreign.

C3: In this case the church not only uses the indigenous language but makes a point of adopting as many religiously neutral cultural norms as possible. The aim is to reduce foreignness as much as possible. Muslim-background believers in the church see themselves as *former* Muslims.

C4: This is similar to C3, but there is a willingness to adopt Islamic religious forms and practices where such are judged biblically permissible: for example, avoiding pork, keeping the fast, praying with raised hands, using more Islamic terms, and so forth. Muslim-background believers still see themselves as *former* Muslims.

C5: In these communities people have accepted Jesus as Lord, as they understand him, and reject elements of Islam that they think are completely incompatible with the Bible, but the list of such incompatibilities is judged pretty short. C5 believers meet with other C5 believers, but they also continue to attend Mosque meetings, read the Qur'an, and revere Muhammad. They are the Muslim equivalent of congregations of Messianic Jews. Most of these converts to Jesus continue to see themselves as Muslims.

C6: These are small groups of converts who meet underground, usually under extreme threat of persecution from totalitarian regimes. Frequently they come to faith in Christ by listening to broadcasts, reading literature, or by contact with Christians while studying abroad. Unlike C5 believers, they keep silent about their faith in the public square, and are viewed by surrounding Muslims as Muslims.

The sweeping debate in missiological circles has centered on C5 communities. Often these are collectively referred to as Insider Movements (hence IM). Many impassioned books and articles have been written on both sides of the debate.[5] Those who support IM feel they are tearing down unnecessary barriers to the conversion of Muslims; those who reject IM feel that the movement is essentially syncretistic and thus a threat to the gospel itself, engendering many spurious conversions. Inevitably, there are numerous mediating positions.

My purpose in mentioning C5 and IM is modest. The IM is an index of the ferment going on about how best to communicate the gospel to Muslims. The debate over how to translate Father-and-Son passages is part of the same ferment. Nevertheless, the two issues must not be completely identified. Supporters of C5 are likely to favor some of the new translations that avoid using Father/Son language, but it does not follow that all those who support these innovative translations favor the Insider Movement. For our purposes we will focus exclusively on the translation issues that have erupted into their own global debates.

---

[5] My own meager contribution to the debate is in a rather lengthy sermon on 1 Corinthians 9:19–23, a passage that supporters of IM frequently cite to justify their position. D. A. Carson, "That By All Means I Might Win Some: Faithfulness and Flexibility in Gospel Presentation" (sermon, The Gospel Coalition 2009 National Conference, April 23, 2009), http://www.thegospelcoalition.org/resources/a/That-By-All-Means-I-Might-Win-Some.

A Bit of History

It is well known that the Qur'an repeatedly denies that Jesus can be thought of as God's Son.[6] At the street level, many Muslims think Christians believe that God somehow impregnated Mary, and that the Trinity is made up of God, Mary, and Jesus, who is thus the Son of God. They find the construct bizarre, not to say blasphemous, and of course they are right. Informed Muslims have a better understanding of what Christians mean by the Trinity, but they find this Christian take on monotheism illogical at best, blasphemous at worst. In short, the objection to thinking of Jesus as the Son of God is not restricted to the repulsiveness of the idea that God had sexual union with a woman, but extends to the deeper criticism of the incarnation: the absolute distinction between God and his creation must not be breached.

Aware of these Muslim sensibilities, some sectors of SIL/ Wycliffe, Frontiers, and other organizations have for a number of years embarked on a variety of Bible translations that have replaced many references to God as the Father and to Jesus as the Son. For example, in one recent Arabic translation, *Al Kalima*, the baptismal formula of Matthew 28 becomes, "Cleanse them by water in the name of Allah, his Messiah and his Holy Spirit."[7] Sometimes "Guardian" has been used instead of "Father." Debates over these steps were confined largely to missionary organizations and journals devoted to the disciplines of Bible translation. Some of those debates were pretty intense. They surged into public view in

---

[6] E.g., 4:171, 172; 5:19, 75–78, 119–120; 9:30–31; 19:35.
[7] For the latest description of *Al Kalima*'s translation policies, which have been considerably revised since the first edition, see http://www.al-kalima.com/translation_project.html.

an article written by Collin Hansen for *Christianity Today*.[8] The report begins with an account of a convert who, while still an unconverted Muslim, first read a Bible that did not refer to Jesus as the "Son of God" but as "the Beloved Son [implicitly of Mary?] who comes (or originates) from God." Sometimes "Son of God" becomes "beloved of God."

Articles and blogposts have proliferated. Biblical Missiology, a ministry of Horizon International, organized a petition against these developments. SIL/Wycliffe has organized study sessions and issued a variety of statements. Toward the end of 2011, its Istanbul statement retreated from the most extravagant renderings while preserving the right to choose less direct renderings wherever there was a danger of suggesting that Father/Son relationships had biological overtones or were based on sexual union. The most recent statement, issued in early February 2012, indicates that all publication of these new translations will be suspended until further discussions have taken place. Frontiers has fostered its own discussions, where it appears that as much time has been spent attempting to maintain good relations and cool the rhetoric as in dealing with the issues of substance. Some churches and denominations have taken public stances against these translational developments (e.g., Overture 9 of the Presbyterian Church of America). Financial support has been cut from some missions or missionaries who back the move away from "Father" and "Son." Occasionally a missionary has left a mission over this issue. Not a few national Christian leaders, themselves Muslim-background believers, working in Arabic, Urdu, Farsi, and other Muslim-majority

---

[8] Collin Hansen, "The Son and the Crescent," *Christianity Today*, Feb. 1, 2011, 18–23.

languages, have taken umbrage at the work of these essentially Western missions, feeling, quite frankly, betrayed.

My own restricted aim in what follows is to offer some evaluations based on what we have so far gleaned from the meaning of "Son of God" as a christological title. I should stipulate two preliminary notes. *First*, because there is no agreed way of referring to these new translations collectively, I shall refer to them as the new translations.[9] *Second*, I shall at several points interact with positions that are no longer held, as well as with current stances, trying to be careful to distinguish between the two. The reason for interaction with positions now eclipsed by more recent discussion is that the translational and theological issues are intrinsically important, and should therefore be borne in mind.

Six Evaluations

(1) We should all recognize the extraordinary diversity of "son of" expressions in the Bible. Probably they should not all be handled the same way. Yet the diversity of ways in which we translate expressions such as "son of oil" and "son of the quiver," mentioned in chapter 1, does not by itself warrant similar diversity in the ways in which we render "son(s) of God."[10]

Consider: Recovering from a cold, someone might say, in English, "I have a frog in my throat." Someone from France would more likely say, in French, "I have a cat in my throat."

---

[9] For a while, some spoke of Muslim Idiom Translations (MIT); others have spoken of translations of divine familial terms. Few are happy with these labels, and I shall avoid them here.

[10] Which is what Rick Brown seems to be advocating in "Part II: Translating the Biblical Term 'Son(s) of God' in Muslim Contexts," *International Journal of Frontier Missiology* 24/4 (2004): 135–45.

(Actually, they say, literally, "I have the cat in the throat"—but we'll let the syntactical difference pass.) How should you render the French "I have a cat in my throat" in English? The obvious answer is to retain the power implicit in a known idiom, and substitute "frog" for "cat." If instead you translate literally, you succeed only in raising the reader's eyebrows, as the French idiom sounds strange in English (as the English idiom sounds strange in French). But suppose the word "cat," within the French text that is being translated, is freighted with many deep and important associations or connotations: what then? Is it wiser to lose the fluency of the idiom while retaining the associations, perhaps with an explanatory footnote, or to retain the fluency of the idiom while losing the associations, perhaps, again, with an explanatory footnote?

"Greet one another with a holy kiss," Paul instructs the Corinthians (1 Cor. 16:20). Literal translation might work well in France and much of the Arab world; it's not going to play very well in China. One understands why J. B. Phillips famously paraphrases, "I should like you to shake hands all round as a sign of Christian love." Probably not much is lost because in the New Testament there are no deep-seated associations connected with kissing; there is, in short, no theology dependent on kissing.

My sister faced another test that has become something of a standard in translation circles. About forty years ago she served as a missionary to a tribe in Papua New Guinea. How does one render, "Look, the Lamb of God, who takes away the sin of the world!" in that context? The people of this tribe had never seen lambs or sheep; they had no word for such animals in their language, and of course had never seen pictures of them. On the other hand, they were accustomed to sacrificing pigs. So would it be wiser to render John 1:29, "Look, the Swine of God who takes away the sin of the world!"? Doubtless one could make a case for such a rendering *provided one abstracted this verse from the rest of Scripture.* But sooner or later Bible translators for this tribe would run into texts that talk about flocks of sheep and fleecing sheep, and still others that designate pork an unclean food not to be eaten by kosher Israelites. What initially seems like an easy fix begins to generate many problems. For there is quite a bit of theology dependent on sheep and pigs.

So how shall we render the biblical "son(s) of" expressions? It seems to do little harm to render "son of the quiver" by "arrow," for referentially that is what is meant, and the Hebrew idiom "son of the quiver" is not transparent when translated literally into English. In other words, this is more like the kissing case than the lamb case! Then how about "son(s) of God"? On almost any reading of the evidence, the associations of the expression are complicated, theologically laden, and inescapable. Why should it not be better, then, to render the original more directly, perhaps with explanatory notes?

(2) In one of his earlier and influential papers, part of which he has since rescinded, Rick Brown, one of the premier thinkers and supporters of the new translations, rightly points out that one of the uses of "Son of God" in the Bible is bound up with the appointment of the Davidic king, the Messiah. In such uses, it is frequently found in parallel with "Messiah."[11] We worked through some of that evidence

---

[11] Rick Brown, "Part 1: Explaining the Biblical Term 'Son(s) of God' in Muslim Contexts," *International Journal of Frontier Missiology* 22/3 (2005): 91–96.

ourselves in the first two chapters. For example, the angel Gabriel tells Mary that Jesus will be called the "Son of the Most High" and will gain the throne of his father David (Luke 1:31–33). The same pair of confessions, that Jesus is the Messiah and that Jesus is the Son of God,[12] is found in 1 John (see, for example, 1 John 5:1, 5). Similarly, we see this in John 1:49, in Nathanael's exclamation, "Rabbi, you are the Son of God, you are the king of Israel"; and again in Galatians 1:11–16, where Paul writes that "the gospel I preached is not of human origin. . . . I received it by revelation from Jesus *Christ*. . . . God . . . was pleased to reveal *his Son* in me." In other words, Brown asserts, Paul takes "Son of God" as "synonymous with 'the Christ.'"[13]

Moreover, Brown goes on to argue that Synoptic parallels point in the same direction. In Peter's confession at Caesarea Philippi, Mark and Luke say, rather simply, that Jesus is "the Messiah" or "God's Messiah" (Mark 8:29; Luke 9:20), while Matthew reports "You are the Messiah, the Son of the living God" (Matt. 16:16). "This establishes," Brown insists in this earlier contribution, "that Jesus and Matthew saw these as synonyms. . . . So 'the Christ' must have been adequate to carry the semantic content of 'Son of God.'"[14] After Saul is converted, "At once he began to preach in the synagogues that Jesus is the Son of God . . . proving that Jesus is the Messiah" (Acts 9:20, 22). Brown again argues, "This shows that proving Jesus is the Christ is adequate to proclaim him to be the Son of God."[15] In short, in Brown's view this reasoning justifies

---

[12] Better: that the Messiah is Jesus and that the Son of God is Jesus.
[13] Brown, "Part I," 94.
[14] Ibid.
[15] Ibid.

substituting "Christ"/"Messiah" for "Son of God" where the latter is likely to cause umbrage. If "Son" causes offense in the Muslim world, then in many passages simply use "Messiah" instead, for that's what "Son" means.

This argument for the "adequacy" of a particular translation is flawed on three grounds. *First*, Brown is of course linguistically informed, and is fully aware that when two expressions are said to be synonymous, it rarely means they are completely interchangeable. If that were the case, then "You are the Messiah, the Son of the living God" really means "You are the Messiah, the Messiah" or, equally, "You are the Son of the living God, the Son of the living God." The two expressions share the same referent, but that does not mean the two expressions mean exactly the same thing. That is apparently why Brown uses "adequacy" terminology in the paper in question: he is presupposing that a shared referent is sufficient warrant for swapping expressions. But a shared referent does not mean that the meanings, associations, and connotations of the two terms are identical. So what is being lost? "Messiah" conjures up anointing, as well as kingly and priestly offices; "Son of God" conjures up family identity, engendering (whether biological or as a metaphor for appointment), a relationship of love, and filial loyalty.

Second, the appeal to Synoptic parallels suggests that when he wrote his paper, Brown had not adequately thought through the issues raised by such parallels. The first is historical: What did Peter actually say? Many utterances in the Gospels do not pretend to be *verbatim* quotations but something akin to accurate summaries. In the case of Peter's confession at Caesarea Philippi, most evangelicals would argue that what Peter actually said was comprehensive enough to include all that Matthew reports; Mark and Luke report less of the total. The second issue is theological: Why do Mark and Luke report less of the total, less than what Matthew reports? Is it because they judge it "adequate" to leave out the "Son of the living God" component, perhaps because they see it as merely redundant? Or is it "adequate" to preserve only "Messiah" and not "Son of the living God" because, while that is "adequate" to establish the referent, their own theological interests and the priorities of their witness find it unnecessary to include every detail of the whole? Almost anyone working constantly in the Gospels would say it is the latter. In other words, their more limited report is "adequate" for their theological purposes. But that means, of course, that for *Matthew's* purposes it is *not* adequate to leave out "Son of the Living God"—and that's why he left the expression in.

Third, Brown's analysis leaves out of consideration the biblical-theological trajectories of the Davidic king motif and of the "Son of God" terminology, trajectories I sketched out in the first two chapters. Biblically informed readers pick up on the associations (e.g., not only, say, 2 Sam. 7:14 and Ps. 2:7, but also Isaiah 9 and Psalms 89 and 110). It is not a responsible riposte to say that the envisaged Muslim readers of the new translations are not biblically informed so they could not conjure up biblical trajectories. That may be true, but it misses the point. For once Bible translations are adopted, they become the standard for the rising Christian community that would then be saddled with translations that fail to preserve these biblical trajectories which make sense of the pattern of the New Testament use of the Old.

Exactly the same sort of response must be advanced when those who defend the new translations observe that in the New Testament the baptismal formula is not always in the name of the Father, the Son, and the Holy Spirit (Matt. 28:19) but is in fact enormously varied (cf. Acts 2:38; 8:12–16; 10:48; 19:3–5; 1 Cor. 6:11). In that same earlier essay, Brown argues, "So when the Trinity was invoked at Baptism, there was flexibility with regard to the way the persons of the Trinity were named."[16] Amen and amen. But it is one thing to observe the diversity found in Scripture and preserve it in our translations, and another thing to appeal to the diversity in Scripture in order to eliminate some of it. If the diverse forms were *exactly* synonymous not only with respect to the referent but also with respect to associations and connotations, this would be an acceptable procedure. Quite demonstrably, however, that is not the case. The result of the logic being deployed is a systematically unfaithful translation.

(3) A great deal of the argument in favor of the new translations is pragmatic. This pragmatism plays out in two ways. Before I list them, it may be helpful to fill in some of the more recent discussion.[17]

In a very recent essay, Rick Brown, Leith Gray, and Andrea Gray have retrenched on one crucial issue, while advancing their case more strongly on others.[18] On the retrenching side, Brown and the Grays, influenced no doubt by the Istanbul consultation (November 2011), demonstrate how "Messiah"

---

[16] Brown, "Part II," 141.
[17] I am grateful to Bryan Harmelink, International Translation Coordinator for SIL International, for helpful exchanges on some of the following points—which of course does not mean he necessarily agrees with all my evaluations.
[18] Rick Brown, Leith Gray, and Andrea Gray, "A New Look at Translating Familial Biblical Terms," *International Journal of Systematic Theology* 28 (2011): 105–20.

and "Son of God" do not have exactly the same meaning even when they share the same referent, and conclude, "We now believe it is ideal to express the familial component of meaning in the text . . . and that terms like "Christ/Messiah" should be used only to translate *Christos/Meshiach* and should not be used to translate *huios/ben*. We would discourage anyone from doing this."[19] Similarly, Wycliffe has posted on its website statements such as these: "Wycliffe USA's policy requires that the eternal deity of Jesus Christ and His relationship with the Father must be preserved in every translation in such a way that communicates [*sic*] accurately and clearly. Wycliffe USA believes that understanding the relationship between God the Father and God the Son, Jesus, is essential to understanding the nature of the Trinity." SIL is attempting to call back some of the new translations that circulated widely before the current and more rigorous standards were adopted.[20] Moreover, since February 2012, SIL/Wycliffe has called a halt to further production of these translations, even under the tighter standards, until further consultation has made clear the way forward.

Nevertheless, this does not mean that SIL/Wycliffe always translates "Father" and "Son," when God and Jesus are the respective referents, in the most direct way. To say that "understanding the relationship between God the Father and God the Son, Jesus, is essential to understanding the nature of the Trinity" is not the same as saying that "Father" and "Son" are categories that must be preserved in translation. The official statement is that *preference* is given to direct translation,

---

[19] Ibid., 116.
[20] See "Divine Familial Terms: Answers to Commonly Asked Questions," Wycliffe Bible Translators, http://www.wycliffe.org/SonofGod/QA.aspx.

but there are many instances, it is argued, when direct translation is in fact misleading, and alternatives must be found in order to preserve the meaning. In fact, most of the lengthy recent essay by Brown and the Grays is devoted to making precisely that point.[21] The difficulty is that so far very few examples have been given of proposed translations of biblical texts where it is deemed best to sidestep the "preference." The stated policy may conceivably be wise and faithful; it sounds a wee bit slippery. It would be helpful at this juncture to have a substantial number of concrete cases to discuss. That brings us to the first of the ways in which the new translators appeal to pragmatic considerations.

(a) It is argued, on the one hand, that traditional renderings are bad translations because for Muslim readers they convey mental images of physical begetting, sexual union, and biological sonship that are deeply offensive to Muslims. This is an important argument, not one to be set aside lightly. If traditional translations convey things that are not true, surely we are duty-bound to do our best to provide translations that do not convey what is false. When experts tell us that the word for "father" in some language or other *means* "begetter," is not this reason enough for abandoning "father"? Or again, Brown and the Grays cite languages where two different words for "son" are used, one meaning a biological child and another meaning a social child (that is, a child belonging to the social unit in some way but not engendered by a stipulated father). Where such words are available, it is surely best, they claim, to use the latter of Jesus the Son of God, rather than the former. In other cases, they advocate "like a son" instead of "son," in

---

[21] Brown et al., "A New Look at Translating Familial Biblical Terms."

much the way that the Targum (an Aramaic paraphrase) to 1 Chronicles 22:10 says, "He will be beloved before me like a son, and I will have compassion on him like a father." This, they acknowledge, is not acceptable in some churches made up of many Muslim-background believers, "because the Father generates the Son non-biologically in eternity and generates his human nature by the virgin Mary. In both cases the Son is generated, but in neither case is procreation involved."[22] A better alternative, in some languages, they say, is "the Son who comes from God" where "comes from" really means "originates from" without any freight of procreation. And surely, they say, some alternative must be found where the word for "father" *means* "begetter."

These approaches are considerably improved over the too-easy substitution of "Messiah" for "Son." Yet apparently on similarly flawed linguistics they are prepared to consider "Beloved" as a substitute, in some cases, for "Son." Moreover, more needs to be said in favor of preserving, in most if not all instances, something closer to traditional renderings. Indeed, for reasons to become clear in a moment, a very good argument can be advanced for *consistent* renderings that reflect "Son" and "Father."

First, although it is difficult for an outsider who does not know the language in question to be certain, one suspects that some of the argumentation is overblown. Does "father" actually *mean* "begetter," or more simply, is it the case that in some language or other "father" is used in very few metaphorical ways so that biological fatherhood is simply assumed? But in that case, might it not be wiser to preserve the biblical imag-

---

[22] Ibid., 115.

ery and include a note to unpack the metaphor, especially if
the price of abandoning the metaphor is as high as we have
seen it to be? Moreover, just because a language does not yet
use a certain metaphor, it does not follow that speakers of
that language cannot understand the metaphor when it is
used, especially if there are some helpful explanatory notes.
The very nature of metaphor is that it enables us to see something in categories normally reserved for something else.[23]

Second, words for "father" and "son" that convey mental pictures of social relationship but not biology may be
as misleading as words for "father" and "son" that convey
mental pictures of a biological connection. For we have seen
how "begetting" or "generation" or "engendering" language
can be used for the way God becomes the "Father" of the
Davidic king, and finally of Jesus himself: that is, the begetting is itself metaphorical. God establishes the Davidide as his
son, he begets him, when the Davidide comes to the throne:
at that point, so far as the activity of reigning is concerned,
the Davidide is to act like his "Father," and thus show himself
to be a true son. This is more than a mere social relationship;
it is a metaphorical engendering. In other words, whatever
word for "son" is chosen in such languages where a choice
is offered, an explanation is going to be needed. In passages
like Psalm 2:7, a socially ordered "son" is as misleading as
a biologically ordered "son." Either translation demands an
explanatory note.

Third, it is often pointed out, correctly, that the deepest
Muslim umbrage is not taken at expressions that have been
falsely understood, but at expressions that have been rightly

---

[23] See the important work of Janet Martin Soskice, *Metaphor and Religious Language*
(Oxford, UK: Oxford University Press, 1985).

understood. The incarnation itself is deeply offensive, however it was brought about. By avoiding language that might make some think of a grotesque sexual union between God and Mary, there is a huge danger that one hides the ready ways in which Jesus is in fact spoken of as God's Son, ways that include his preexistence, his relationship with the Father in eternity past, his becoming a human being while still remaining God, and so forth.[24]

Fourth, the new translations strike some of us as an undisciplined form of reader-response theory applied now to Bible translation. In chapter 1 I briefly alluded to the recent work of Michael Peppard on the Son of God.[25] Among other things, Peppard argues that "son of God" may have conjured up Davidic ideology in one audience, tales of Greek gods in another, and the Roman Emperor in another. He fastens on the Roman Emperor because this, he thinks, is what a Roman audience would call to mind, and "this resonance affects our understanding of the Gospel of Mark and other selected Christian texts."[26] The problem with Peppard's approach is that he then reads back into Mark what he thinks would be conjured up in the minds of Romans by the expression "son of God," *without wrestling with what Mark actually says on Mark's terms*. Peppard is right to point out that initially the expression "son of God" by itself might conjure up different things to different audiences, but neither Mark nor any other

---

[24] As Robert Yarbrough puts it in Hansen's article, "This is a key point where the nature of God vis-à-vis creation is just categorically different in the two religions. In one, God is utterly transcendent and unknowable and without peer or parallel of any kind in creation. He is, quite simply, inscrutable; we cannot call him 'Father' and so forth. The God of Abraham and of David and of Jesus is not like this. The 'Son of God' language in the New Testament is the tip of an iceberg" ("The Son and the Crescent," 23).

[25] Michael Peppard, *The Son of God in the Roman World: Divine Sonship in Its Social and Political Context* (Oxford, UK: Oxford University Press, 2011).

[26] Ibid., 28.

New Testament writer is so plastic in his handling of "Son of God" themes that it is either right or fair to ignore the fact that the biblical writers themselves are making an argument. Thus to a reader who connects the expression "Son of God" with royal Davidic themes, Matthew 22:41–46 introduces expansive categories to show that the Messiah is *more* than David's son.

Again, John's Gospel happily associates Messiah and Son of God, but a passage like John 5:16–30, as we have seen, so deepens what it means to affirm that Jesus is the Son of God that our entire understanding of God and of sonship are enriched and transformed. *This is not a mere translational matter. No language, no culture, means by "Son" what Jesus means in John 5—yet "Son" is the category Jesus uses, even though nothing in English, or Urdu, or Arabic, prepares us for a Son of God whose relationship with the Father is anything like what the text describes.* All of us—English speakers in London or New York or Baton Rouge, Urdu speakers in Karachi, Arabic speakers in Heliopolis, Kresh speakers in Africa—are *necessarily* linguistically unprepared for such a vision of God as this. If English seems to accommodate it today, it is simply because of the long heritage of Bible reading. Yet as our culture becomes increasingly biblically illiterate, we are going to have to start all over again to explain the various things the Bible means when it instructs us to confess that Jesus is the Son of God. The new Bible translators are in danger of using reader-response theory to domesticate the Scriptures, much the way Peppard does, instead of allowing Scripture to challenge the antecedent cultural understanding.

At the very least we must constantly be vigilant, not least in Bible translation, with the argument that some culture or other can or cannot accept this or that. At its best, the argument enables us to translate wisely and prudently; at its worst, it becomes an excuse for unwittingly removing from the message itself things that are clearly taught in the Bible and are therefore simply nonnegotiable.

(b) The second pragmatic appeal is that the success of these new translations is so remarkable that, as the old expression puts it, the proof of the pudding is in the eating. It is hard to test the figures that circulate, but thousands have been converted, in some sense, through these new translations. Yet when certain tests are made, 46 percent of such converts avow that they prefer to read the Qur'an than the Bible, 72 percent continue to think of Muhammad as the final prophet, and so forth.[27] How many of the conversions are spurious? If it is argued (and it is) that we have many spurious conversions in the West, too, that point is readily conceded. Yet arguably, in the West such spurious conversions turn, in large part, on shallow preaching, bad handling of the Scriptures, little spiritual discernment among many pastors and preachers, and lack of courage in the actual handling of the Bible. Moreover the large number of spurious conversions in the West is widely viewed as a weakness of our evangelism and Bible teaching, a weakness to be challenged and corrected. What is being advocated by some of the new translators is that a parallel weakness be worked back from poor teaching *into the Bible*

---

[27] See, for example, Phil Parshall, "Danger! New Directions in Contextualization," *Evangelical Missions Quarterly* 34 (1998): 404–6, 409–10; and discussion by Timothy C. Tennent, "Followers of Jesus (Isa) in Islamic Mosques: A Closer Examination of C-5 'High Spectrum' Contextualization," *International Journal of Frontier Missiology* 23 (2006): 101–15.

translations themselves, and then warmly embraced. This sounds like a recipe for disaster.

(4) One of the things I have tried to demonstrate in the previous two chapters is that distinguishable uses of "Son of God" can be used side by side, *held together by nothing more than the expression itself*, with the result that the entire conception of "Son of God" is enriched. I shall remind you of four examples.

(a) In Matthew 1–4, Jesus is the Son of God in that, like Israel the son of God, he recapitulates much of Israel's experience—in being called out of Egypt and in being tempted and tested in the wilderness for forty days and nights. But the latter event is preceded by the declaration of the voice from heaven at Jesus's baptism, "This is my Son, whom I love" (3:17)—almost certainly picking up on the Davidic/kingly use of sonship, which in any case is certainly further developed in Matthew's Gospel. There is no point in asking, "OK, then, which kind of son is he really?" The point is that Jesus is the perfect Israel *and* the perfect David, and the two notions are held together by the one rubric, Son of God.

(b) We observed that in Hebrews 1:5–13, "Son of God" is heavily tied to the Davidic line. Nevertheless, readers cannot and should not try to escape from the influence of the "Son" in the previous verses (Heb. 1:1–4), where the Son is preexistent, God's agent in the creation of the universe, the radiance of God's glory, the one who currently upholds everything by his sovereign word after making an atoning sacrifice for sin, and so forth. This "Son" usage is common enough in the New Testament, and finds its roots in the Old Testament (e.g., Isaiah 9). My point, however, is that the writer to the

Hebrews so brings the two uses of "Son" together that it is unwise, if not impossible, to read verses 5–13 without being influenced by verses 1–4. One of the results is that while the address to the Davidic monarch in Psalm 45, "Your throne, O God, will last for ever and ever," may be taken as hyperbolic for various contextually important reasons, when it is here applied to Jesus it is *not* meant to be hyperbolic but simply true, for equally contextually important reasons. And all of this is held together not only by Scripture's Davidic typology *but also by the manner in which the writer to the Hebrews in one chapter brings together two analytically differentiable uses of "Son" terminology.* If one of these uses of "Son" is lost in translation, the thematic linking is also lost.

(c) We have already seen how, in the birth announcement to Mary, the "Son of the Most High" will receive the throne of his father David (Luke 1:29–37). So in this context, "Son" is linked to Jesus's accession to the Davidic throne. In fact, the text displays a more complex interplay of themes, for we are also told that the *reason* that the holy one to be born of Mary will be called the Son of God is that the power of the Most High will overshadow her. We are dealing with the most intimate mysteries surrounding the incarnation. None of this was true of any other Davidide. It was not until they came to the throne that God "begat" these other Davidides, that he became their Father. In some contexts that is true of Jesus: he enters his reign at a particular point, perhaps, as we've seen, at his resurrection/ascension. But here the *reason* Jesus is called the Son of God is the virginal conception brought about by the mysterious brooding power of the Most High. To eliminate "Son of God" from either one of these uses blinds the reader to the way that Jesus is the Son of God in both senses. And once again it is the "Son" terminology that holds them together.

(d) We have observed that according to John 20:30–31 the purpose of the fourth Gospel is to commend Jesus as the Messiah, the Son of God. Here is the same Messiah/King/Son concatenation with which we are familiar. But this assertion of the purpose of the Fourth Gospel occurs after passages like John 5:16–30, where the Son's extraordinary relationship to his heavenly Father is spelled out in categories that constitute part of the groundwork for the doctrine of the Trinity. Much of what holds all this together, once again, is the "Son" terminology.

In other words, the richest theological loading of the expression "Son of God" as applied to Jesus springs from passages that deploy the expression *to cross-pollinate distinctive uses.* This fact constitutes a driving reason to translate "Son of God" and "Father" expressions consistently, for otherwise these crucial intracanonical links will be lost to view.

(5) Perhaps a personal word here will not go amiss. I have had the privilege of working with SIL/Wycliffe personnel on three continents. I am a huge admirer of their work, some of it undertaken in highly challenging circumstances. Some of them are linguistically well trained. But I have to say that rather few of them are trained in exegesis, biblical theology, or systematic theology. Very few of them have an MDiv, let alone more advanced training. With rare exceptions, I have not found them to be deep readers of Scripture, with the result that their approaches to translation challenges tend to be atomistic. No one can be an expert in everything, of

course—but if I have any hope for this book, it is that some of these diligent and learned workers will begin to see the importance for Bible translation of the considerations I am advancing here, and that more of them will pursue advanced theological training as part of their preparation for a life in translation.

(6) My last evaluative comment has little to do, directly, with Bible translation, but merely brings together three observations. *First*, the new approach to Bible translation is in danger of cutting off its "converts" from the history of the confessionalism of the universal church. It is not a light thing to stand so aloof from the authority of those early councils and creeds that reflect so much sustained thought regarding how to think about God. This does not mean that those early councils and creeds necessarily got everything right. Nevertheless, the kind of biblicism that learns nothing from the great councils is in danger of becoming cultic. *Second*, a considerable literature has arisen from Muslim-convert believers who are aghast at these developments, arguing on both technical and personal grounds that these new translations are the product of Westerners who are imposing their work on local churches. It is difficult to be certain how much of this is grounded in informed criticism and how much is mere cultural conservatism. So far, however, I have not detected much pastoral sensitivity to this point on the part of some new translation theorists. *Third*, the spread of the gospel in the early church saw the dissemination of Scripture *along with the provision of missionaries and pastors.* One wonders if at least some of the tensions over Bible translation springs from the commitment on the part of some to provide

adequate translations without simultaneously providing missionaries and pastors.

To be frank, it would be good to see less energy devoted to taking us away from the theological richness of the multifaceted biblical affirmations of Jesus's sonship, and much more energy expended on understanding and then learning how to teach all that the Bible does and does not say about Jesus the Son of God. Then those who are genuinely converted will stand with Christians across centuries and cultures, and quietly and reverently affirm, "I believe in God the Father Almighty, Maker of heaven and earth, and in his only Son Jesus, our Lord."

GENERAL INDEX

SCRIPTURE INDEX